D1014462

AGGRESSION

AGGRESSION
The Myth of the Beast Within

John Klama

John Klama is a pseudonym. This book has been edited by John Durant, Peter Klopfer and Susan Oyama from a text coauthored by John Durant, Erika Honoré, Lisa Klopfer, Martha Klopfer, Peter Klopfer, Tamara Kohn, Bryan Lessley, Nadav Nur, and Susan Oyama

John Wiley & Sons, Inc.
New York

John Wiley & Sons, Inc.
605 Third Avenue,
New York, NY 10158, United States of America

*Copublished with Longman Scientific & Technical,
Longman Group UK Limited, Longman House,
Burnt Mill, Harlow, Essex CM20 2JE, England*

First published 1988

Library of Congress Cataloging-in-Publication Data
Klama, John.
The myth of the beast within.

Written by John Durant, Peter Klopfer, and Susan
Oyama under joint pseudonym John Klama, based on
contributions by J. Durant . . . [et al.].
Bibliography: p.
Includes index.
1. Aggressiveness (Psychology) 2. Psychobiology.
3. Socialpsychology. I. Title.
BF575.A3K53 1988 302.5′4 87-2765
ISBN 0-470-20790-6 (USA only)

Set in 10/12pt Plantin Comp/Edit 6400
Produced by Longman Singapore Publishers (Pte) Ltd.
Printed in Singapore.

Contents

Preface

In the summer of 1980, in a small chateau in the south of France, a group of scientists gathered to discuss what they knew, thought they knew, or wished they knew about aggression. Apart from the relaxed sun-and-wine ambience, this scientific conference differed little from others of its kind: there was a great deal of lecturing; and even more questioning and discussion. One particular speaker, however, almost hypnotized the assembled company with a powerful discourse on the control of behaviour. He described patients in his care who suffered from episodes of uncontrollable aggressive rage; and he told how, by implanting miniaturized, computerized electrodes into particular areas of the brain, he could pick up signals that enabled him to anticipate and in turn to prevent such outbursts.

The computer-controlled patient whose photograph we were shown looked like any other person on the streets of his city; and as we gazed at him, the prospect of seemingly normal people being 'steered' by a microelectronic 'stimoceiver' enthralled us all. But fleetingly at first, and then in a wave, many of us were overcome, not just by the realization of what one particular kind of biological study of aggression had already led to in the present, but even more by the awful prospect of what such an enterprise could so easily lead to in the future.

For many of us, science is an intensely personal affair. It is not only a profession but also a vocation, in the ecclesiastical sense. Vocations, however, often generate an evangelical fervour; and such fervour may come to embrace the passionate desire not merely to change the world, which is laudable, but to control it, which is not. More than anything else, our conference had exposed the depths of our present ignorance about aggression. Continually, we had been faced with the enormous complexity of aggressive behaviour, as well as with the many gaps and apparent contradictions in the scientific evidence relating to it.

How, then, in the case of our lecturer's patients, could we be so sure that we knew precisely what their problems were? And why should we presume that the solution to these problems lay with surgical intrusions into the brain and the implantation of a little microelectronic gadgetry?

Above all, what were the conceptions of human nature and human dignity that had led us even to consider the use of 'stimoceivers' as an appropriate medical treatment?

Those of us who were present at that lecture on human behaviour control were uneasy, both about our own enthrallment with the idea of the remote control of human aggression, and about others' apparent willingness to acclaim it as a valuable contribution to behavioural science and psychiatry. We decided to face up to this unease by reviewing the question of the 'biology of aggression'. What is the true extent of current scientific understanding in this field; and how far does such understanding provide a legitimate basis for some of the more ambitious programmes aimed at resolving problems of personal and social conflict 'scientifically'?

From these beginnings, a small group was assembled, drawn from anthropology, biology, history, political science, and psychology. We met individually, in threes, fours, and *en masse* on several occasions over a period of around two years. In between meetings, we exchanged views on mountains of paper and during lengthy phone calls. Out of all this emerged a manuscript, each chapter of which was a distinctive contribution by just one or two of us that nevertheless attempted to take into account the views of the others. That manuscript, however, is not what you see here. For in order to achieve an integrity that many separate writers cannot achieve, three of us undertook to rewrite the whole and prepare it for publication.

We all felt that the work in the various fields from which we came was often compromised by scientists' failure to examine basic issues carefully and critically. In addition to the questions of clinical practice mentioned above, we had all been disturbed by the ease and the frequency with which particular aspects of our lives were being commented upon in the name of science. Over and again, this or that feature of daily life was pronounced 'biological', 'innate', or 'instinctive'; and from this, it was often concluded that the feature was 'natural', hard to change, or even inevitable. If the feature in question was a source of pleasure or security, of course, well and good; but if it was a source of pain or danger, then only drugs, electrodes, or genetic engineering might suffice to put things right.

On this view, it seemed that biology dealt only with the fixed and unalterable aspects of our lives, leaving everything else to other branches of the human sciences. Apparently, the biological sciences offered little more than a series of boundaries or constraints within which we were obliged to live out our lives. But was this really so? From the outset, we were sure that biology had far more to offer than this; and as our work proceeded, we became more and more convinced of the importance of articulating clearly what was wrong with the prevailing images of the biological and the social in our culture. There are considerable dangers in unreflectiveness in this area; for a culture that looks to the biological (or any other) sciences for answers to momentous questions needs to be acutely aware of the ways in which these sciences may draw upon, and hence perpetuate, everyday common-or-garden prejudices about human affairs.

In writing this book, we have been obliged to confront the many different meanings of biology, both in our science and in our culture. We are aware that others have attempted before to clarify some of the confusions that so persistently surround this and related terms. In the United States, for example, the biologist T. C. Schnierla (1956, 1966) and many of his students, including Danny Lehrman (1953, 1970), pioneered the critical examination of the biological concept of instinct; and in Britain, Robert Hinde (1960), Patrick Bateson (1982, 1983) and Richard Dawkins (1982) have worked in a similarly thoughtful way in the areas of motivation, development, and evolution. In looking at the conceptions of the 'biological basis' of aggression that have been dominant in our culture for a very long time, we have tried to continue in the tradition of this critical literature.

We came to this project as academics and as ordinary people, with a mixture of overlapping intellectual and practical concerns. We knew many of the tales that people had been tempted to tell, and many of the things that clinicians had been tempted to do, in the name of biology. We had heard the biological stories of inherent natures resistant to change, of single destinies, and of ineluctable fates; and we had seen the clinical attempts to correct or control all manner of behavioural 'pathology' with drugs, electrodes, or scalpels. At the same time, we knew that these ways of theorizing and treating human behaviour regularly provoked fierce opposition from those who insisted that this or that human behavioural characteristic was not biological at all, but cultural; and we knew how sterile had become this apparently endless battle of the biological versus the social, nature versus nurture.

The questions we have asked of one another over the past few years have become the basis of this book: How have biological studies of aggression come to be pitted against other scientific approaches to the same phenomena in a war of conflicting explanations and predictions? How can biological studies of aggression be reconceived in such a way that this no longer happens? How can the exuberant variety of human life be joined with its communality and its orderliness without at the same time sacrificing the integrity of human experience by doling out some parts of it to biology and others to the social sciences? How can the richness and the diversity upon which all biology is based be fully incorporated into our view of human conflict? How, in short, can biology be made to tell different stories from the ones it has so often been made to tell in the past?

1987

John Durant
Peter Klopfer
Susan Oyama

About the authors

John Durant studied zoology and history of science at the University of Cambridge. Since then, he has worked in continuing education, first at the University College of Swansea in Wales, and then in the Department for External Studies at the University of Oxford. His primary interests are in behavioural, evolutionary, and human biology, and he researches widely on the history, philosophy, and social relations of these subjects.

Erika Honoré did graduate work in animal behaviour at the University of North Carolina, and then took up veterinary medicine. She has co-authored a text on animal behaviour, and continues to combine veterinary work with the training and study of horses.

Lisa Klopfer was introduced to anthropology at Bryn Mawr College, Pennsylvania and this led to graduate studies at the University of Pennsylvania and fieldwork in Indonesia. She is particularly interested in the role of food in the integration of social behaviour.

Martha Klopfer studied the theory of moral education and development at Duke University and currently participates in these processes at Carolina Friends School. She has collaborated extensively with Peter Klopfer in studies of mother–infant relations, which is another field in which she has extensive practical experience.

Peter Klopfer trained as a zoologist at Yale and Cambridge Universities. He has worked on various aspects of behavioural ecology and behaviour development, and is the author and editor of several major texts in these fields. His primary interests of late have been in the establishment of mother–infant relations and the control of aggression. He is a member of the Zoology Department at Duke University.

Tamara Kohn began her studies of anthropology at the University of California, Berkeley, and went on to do graduate work at the University of Pennsylvania and Somerville College, Oxford. Her work on the Isle of Coll in the Inner Hebrides off the west coast of Scotland focuses on the seasonality of events, ethnohistory, and notions of identity.

Bryan Lessley was trained in history at Duke University, went on to study law at Harvard University, and is now a practising attorney. At Harvard, he was particularly interested in environmental law, but his current interests span a wide range of social issues.

Nadav Nur began his research on alternative breeding strategies at Duke University, and then continued them at Oxford, Stirling, and Tübingen, where he currently holds a research fellowship in the Institüt für Biologie. He has done extensive fieldwork on the breeding biology of birds, though his interests are focused upon theoretical issues in behavioural ecology.

Susan Oyama studied social psychology at Harvard. She has taught at Sarah Lawrence College in New York and the John Jay College of Criminal Justice, City University of New York, where she is currently a professor of psychology. Her primary interest is in the critical reappraisal of major concepts in the biological and the social sciences. Her book, *The Ontogeny of Information: Developmental Systems and Evolution*, was published in 1985.

Acknowledgements

All of us have incurred considerable debts in the writing of this book. Since ours is a joint work, we shall not list separate acknowledgements by individual author. Instead, we should like collectively to convey our thanks to David Benton, Leslie Carlin, Margie Happel, Stuart Kirsch, Rosemary Morlin, E. I. Schieffelin, and Don Wells for help at various stages in the project. Nicholas Thompson, Ethel Tobach, and a third anonymous reviewer were all extremely generous in making constructive criticisms of the text; and our editor, Michael Rodgers, was extremely patient in coping with the tribulation of having not one author to deal with, but nine. During the early stages of manuscript preparation, Nadav Nur was supported by a NATO postdoctoral fellowship in science at the Biological Sciences Department, University of Stirling, Scotland.

The publishers are grateful to the following copyright holders for permission to reproduce copyright material:

Cambridge University Press for our fig 7.1 from fig 1 p 256 (Lorenz 1950); Editions Mengés and Richard Dawkins for our fig 2.2 from the front cover of the French paperback edition of (Dawkins 1976), *Le gène égoïste* (1978); *The Daily Mail* for our fig 2.1; the James Arthur Committee, American Museum of Natural History, New York, for our fig 7.4 adapted from a photograph in (Delgado 1965); Springer-Verlag Heidelberg and Richard Dawkins for our fig 2.2 from the front cover of the German paperback edition of (Dawkins 1976), *Das egoistische Gen* (1978).

Guggenheim Foundation has supported Peter Klopfer's work.

CHAPTER ONE

On aggression

Introduction

The supposedly 'advanced' western industrial societies have come to see conflict as a basic fact of life. However much they may long for harmony within communities and peace among the nations, our societies are haunted by the spectre of violence. Newspapers, radio, and television alarm readers and audiences with an apparently endless series of reports – of chronically high levels of child abuse and marital violence within the home; of fighting on the streets, at the workplace, and in sports stadia; of terrorist outrages in airports and discotheques; and of wars and rumour of wars. And as if all this were not enough, everyone faces (or, more likely, turns away from) the appalling and mind-numbing possibility of a nuclear conflict between the superpowers. In this last sense, in particular, the western world – the whole world – finds itself living *In a Dark Time* (Humphrey and Lifton 1984).

The English language contains many different words with which to voice a concern about conflict. 'Threat' is one, and 'violence' is another; but a third, and perhaps the most powerful of all, is 'aggression'. Applicable equally to the behaviour of individuals, social groups, and political alliances, aggression is anything and everything from the petulance of a frustrated child to the polemics of a superpower leader. It is what people say (as in, 'she adopted an aggressive tone of voice'), what they do (as in, 'he committed an act of aggression'), and why they do it (as in, 'she gave way to an aggressive impulse'). Aggression is something that everyone has – or is meant to have – albeit in varying amounts; supposedly, football players have a great deal, business people have just the right amount, and mothers and mystics have very little indeed. For many of those who have come to regard conflict as a fact of life, people are just 'naturally aggressive'.

This book is about aggression – the word itself, and the cluster of facts and theories, ideas and opinions, hopes and fears that have come to surround it both in our society and in our science. Like most other words, aggression is primarily an unanalysed term in ordinary speech; but secondarily, it is also a technical term in the scientific analysis of animal and human behaviour. One of the things this book considers is the interplay between the popular and the scientific meanings of aggression. It argues that much scientific analysis of aggression tends to reflect and, in turn, to reinforce popular beliefs in our culture about the intractability or even the inevitability of conflict; and it suggests that the time has come to change this gloomy cycle of fatalistic influence. The science and politics of conflict need not be about the management of our inevitable aggression, nor yet about the domestication of our innate 'beastliness'; it could be about the creation of more opportunities for the constructive resolution of conflict, or about the maximization of our 'beastly' potential for other than so-called 'beastly' behaviour. The theme of this book is that the time has come to change both the scientific image and the social reality of aggression.

The aggression debate

Over the past 25 years, the scientific study of aggression has grown to become a major branch of the behavioural sciences. To a large extent, this growth has been fuelled by public and political concern about violence. In the 1960s, problems as varied as the growth of violent crime, the Vietnam War, the increasing significance of various forms of civil disobedience, and the continuing escalation of the nuclear arms race all served to encourage research on animal and human conflict. In the early 1970s, the volume of work going on in this area continued to grow quite rapidly; and in 1977, two prominent contributors summed up very neatly the self-image of their expanding field: 'Along with the explosion of violence', they wrote, 'there has been an explosion of literature on the problem of violence' (Crabtree and Moyer 1977).

A good example of the interaction between public and scientific interest in aggression is provided by the discovery in the 1960s of a human chromosomal abnormality known as the XYY syndrome. This condition involves the inheritance by men of an extra Y or male chromosome. Like so many findings relating to human genetics, this one created an enormous amount of interest. In retrospect, it is not difficult to see why there was so much fuss. Much of the early work on the syndrome was done with inmates of mental and penal institutions, including men with a history of violence; and some researchers were inclined to see the extra chromosome as a contributing cause of these men's antisocial behaviour. This was more than enough for the popular press, which seized upon the condition as evidence for the existence of what *Newsweek* referred to as 'Congenital Criminals'. In this way, scientists and their popularizers combined to create the impression that biology was helping to diagnose and cure pressing social problems. Indeed, one group of researchers involved in this work called explicitly for 'applied research aimed at curbing unnecessary and excessive violence' (Jarvik, Klodin, and Matsuyama 1973).

The political motivation of much aggression research makes it the subject of more-or-less continuous and occasionally bitter argument. Politics is about the ordering of relationships in society, and hence it is about alternative ideals and ideologies by which to live. Clearly, such alternatives are controversial; indeed, they are precisely the kind of thing over which people may become aggressive in their attempts to settle their differences. Thus, the appeal to science for assistance in the resolution of political problems inevitably plunges scientists into the public arena of conflict over values; and this is what has happened time and again within the field of aggression research.

Consider once again, for example, the case of the so-called XYY syndrome. Following the announcement of a possible link between possession of an extra Y chromosome and certain forms of criminal violence, Dr Stanley Walzer at the Boston Hospital for Women began screening all newborn babies with a view to long-term follow-up of the behaviour of affected males. This screening programme met with fierce criticism from several scientists who were members of an organization called Science for the People. These critics objected that it was wrong to label, and thus risk stigmatizing for life, baby boys who happened to be born with an extra Y chromosome. Denouncing as unproven the hypothesized link between XYY and criminality, they dismissed the idea of a genetic basis for antisocial behaviour as a dangerous myth (Elseviers 1974; Beckwith 1976; Pyeritz et al. 1977). After months of acrimonious debate, and in response to what two commentators have described as 'frightening personal pressures', Walzer voluntarily ended his screening programme in 1975.

The Boston XYY research programme has been described as an example of 'How Not to Study Violence' (Powledge 1981). But it is typical of a large number of studies that have begun as scientific analyses of aggression and ended as bitter political wrangles. Other well-known examples in recent years include: ethological explorations of animal and human aggression (Lorenz 1966; Montagu 1968); sociobiological inquiries into the evolution of conflict (Wilson 1975; Caplan 1978; Rose, Lewontin, and Kamin 1984); and physical, chemical, and psychological investigations of disorderly, disruptive, or violent human subjects (Mark and Ervin 1970; Wender 1971; Valenstein 1974, 1986; O'Callaghan and Carroll 1981). Almost wherever natural scientists have investigated human aggression, the results have been hotly disputed.

Obviously, each particular dispute involves detailed questions of evidence and interpretation, and many of these will be taken up in due course. But underlying all of the details there are three fundamental and interrelated questions that have persistently divided workers in this field: First, what is aggression? Secondly, what are the respective roles of the biological and the social sciences in the study of aggression? Thirdly, what is the relationship between the scientific study of aggression and the social reality of human conflict? Overwhelmingly, it is because students of aggression hold differing views on one or all of these questions that they find themselves disagreeing over matters of technical fact or theory. Each of these questions crops up repeatedly throughout the book; but by considering them briefly at the outset, it is hoped both to clarify our terms of reference and to introduce some of our major themes.

What is aggression?

What, exactly, is meant by the term 'aggression'? This has been an abiding preoccupation in the technical literature. Indeed, at times workers have abandoned scientific for purely semantic inquiry (see, for example, van der Dennen 1980). This is unfortunate. Obviously, it is vital in any field of academic inquiry that words be used properly. However, at the end of the day words mean what they are taken to mean; and what they are taken to mean is largely a matter of custom. Definitions are not either true or false; rather, they are either useful or useless. What, then, is a useful way of using the term aggression?

In ordinary speech, the label 'aggressive' is applied very widely as a description of all sorts of conduct in which individuals or groups of individuals actively pursue their interests against each other in society. Thus, athletes, politicians, society hostesses, business corporations, and nation-states may all be termed aggressive if they promote themselves against their rivals abrasively or vigorously enough. Obviously, this sort of vernacular usage embraces an enormously wide range of activities that may share little in common at the behavioural level – apart, perhaps, from a general quality of assertiveness.

Many behavioural scientists are distrustful of theoretical terms that cannot be translated into precise behavioural measures, and for this (among other) reasons they tend to reject the vernacular in favour of narrower, more technical definitions of aggression. Typically, their efforts have come to focus on the notion of aggression as individual behaviour directed towards causing physical injury to others (see, for example, Hinde 1974). Several comments may be made about this technical definition. First, the focus is on the individual as the object of interest. On this usage, which appears to differ sharply from the vernacular, it is not social groups or institutions but only their members (or representatives) who may be described as aggressive.

A second feature of the technical definition is that it is functional. To establish whether behaviour is directed towards causing physical injury to others we have to know what behaviour is for; and knowing what behaviour is for is knowing its function. On this view, behaviour whose function is to cause physical injury to others, but which fails to achieve this aim, is nonetheless aggressive; whereas behaviour whose function is not to cause physical injury, but which happens to do so by accident, is not aggressive. Here, technical usage appears to fit rather well with the vernacular.

A third point about the technical definition is that it appears to exclude many kinds of behaviour that are commonly termed aggressive, even in the technical literature, but whose function appears to be merely the withdrawal of another individual rather than its physical injury. If one individual threatens another, for example, common sense tells us that this may be an aggressive act; but if the threatened individual retreats, no physical injury may be attempted. This point can be met by modifying the technical definition to read: aggression is behaviour directed towards causing, or threatening to cause, physical injury to others.

Finally, there remains the problem of what is to count as physical injury. Although at first sight this seems clear enough, a moment's reflection reveals that some tricky distinctions may be in order. For example, is the injury caused by parasites to their hosts, or predators to their prey, to be termed aggression? Most scientists agree that these phenomena are special cases. Some prefer to make them special cases of aggression, while others prefer to adopt a different analytic category altogether; and a decision between these alternatives will depend as much upon the particular context of inquiry as anything else.

For most scientific studies of animal aggression, something approximating to the modified technical definition of aggression given above will usually suffice. The closer we get to humans, however, the more difficult it becomes to do justice to the complexity of the behavioural interactions that may be involved. In our own case, we know that the aims or intentions underlying our behaviour are enormously subtle and varied. We know, also, that the threat or performance of physical injury is only one – and not by any means always the most effective – way of asserting oneself in the face of an actual or a potential rival. As we have already seen, everyday speech recognizes this fact by extending the use of the term aggression to cover a very wide range of more-or-less assertive acts. This is perfectly acceptable, so long as we are always careful to remember exactly which meaning of aggression we are using at any particular time.

The importance of this last caution can scarcely be overemphasized. The very fact that we possess a single term in our language that is capable of being applied to anything and everything from stag fights to star-wars is a trap for the unwary. For it tempts them to regard aggression, not as a category of convenience, but rather as a natural class of phenomena. Of course, there are natural classes of phenomena. 'Bird' and 'mammal' are two such classes, in the sense that they refer to groups of organisms that we have good reason to believe are biologically distinct. Birds and mammals possess unique distinguishing features, and in placing animals in these categories we are, so to speak, carving nature at the joints. Our confidence that this is so comes from the theory of evolution, which tells us that birds and mammals are separate branches on the tree of life.

There is no reason in principle why behavioural phenomena should not fall into natural classes of this kind. Certain kinds of display movements among birds, for example, share unique distinguishing features by virtue of common evolutionary ancestry; and by bringing them together under a common term we are identifying fundamental and natural rather than superficial and artificial divisions. This is not the case, however, with the phenomena that we bring together (either in everyday speech, or even – for the most part – in technical science) under the label aggression. In this case, as will become evident later in this book, we are almost certainly dealing with a multiply-evolved and extraordinarily diverse group of behavioural phenomena. In this situation, it is not safe to presume anything about the underlying nature(s), cause(s), and function(s) of the interactions that we choose to label aggressive in advance of thorough scientific investigation.

We have dwelt on this rather abstract point because in the past many investigators have fallen into the trap of presuming that simply because the term aggression is applied to a large number of different activities in everyday life these must all belong to the same natural class. Indeed, this intuition drawn from the world of everyday affairs constitutes one of the most significant ways in which wider society has left its mark on scientific investigations of animal and human conflict. For, once accept that the label aggression refers to a natural class of behaviour patterns, and it is but a short step to the conclusion that beneath the superficially diverse range of phenomena embraced by the term there lies a unitary biological 'base' – an aggressive 'instinct', perhaps, whose origins may be traced far back in animal evolution.

Thus, the psychiatrist Anthony Storr, essaying to define the place of an 'aggressive instinct' in human life, notes that, 'the words we use to describe intellectual effort are aggressive words. We *attack* problems, or *get our teeth into* them. We *master* a subject when we have *struggled with* and *overcome* its difficulties'; and, on these grounds, Storr concludes that 'The aggressive part of human nature . . . is the basis of intellectual achievement, and even of that proper pride which enables a man to hold his head high amongst his fellows' (Storr 1970, p. 11). What Storr has done here is to infer a common underlying nature from the common use of aggressive labels; he has been seduced by everyday language to the point where he simply assumes what he ought to – but cannot – demonstrate; namely, that there is a single ('instinctive') motivational source for all the things that people customarily term aggressive.

Biological and social studies of aggression

Our discussion of definitions has brought us to the second of our three questions; namely, what is the relationship between biological and social approaches to aggression? This question is part of a much larger controversy that has raged with varying degrees of intensity for well over a century. On the one side, there is the claim that human behaviour is partly or wholly determined by human biology; on the other, there is the counter-claim that human behaviour is largely or wholly independent of human biology, being instead the product of exclusively social influences. In recent years, the contest between these two (greatly oversimplified) positions has become more than usually fierce, with the champions of biology pitting themselves against those of society in what has gradually taken on the appearance of a war of attrition.

Consider by way of illustration a recent critique of biological approaches to human behaviour by Steven Rose, Leon Kamin, and Richard Lewontin (1984). Under the title *Not in Our Genes*, this book condemns biological analyses of everything from aggression to xenophobia in humans as the expression of a false and pernicious philosophy that it dubs 'biological determinism'. Biological determinism is the doctrine that human behaviour is the direct and unalterable expression of a 'genetically based' human nature. Rose, Kamin, and Lewontin reject such a view. Instead, they prefer a perspective in which human biology is only trivially relevant to human behaviour, since society itself generates most or all of the significant patterns of behavioural interaction in which scientists take an interest.

In defending this latter position, Rose, Kamin, and Lewontin cast aside whole areas of behavioural biology as being of little or no scientific value. For example, they dismiss sociobiology (a major branch of contemporary evolutionary theory) as 'vulgar Mendelism, vulgar Darwinism, and vulgar reductionism in the service of the status quo'. The reaction from those whose work has been so roundly condemned is, perhaps, predictable. One English sociobiologist, for example, who has been the object of particular criticism ever since the publication of his popular book *The Selfish Gene* (1976), has dismissed his critics with open contempt. According to Richard Dawkins, *Not in Our Genes* is 'a silly, pretentious, obscurantist and mendacious book' (Dawkins 1985).

What are bystanders to make of this longstanding feud? To judge from much of the literature that still pours forth on one side or the other of the debate, they appear to be faced with a stark choice between biology and the social sciences. More particularly, they seem to have to choose between 'nature' and 'nurture' – or, at least, between one mixture of both influences and another. The contrast between nature and nurture is familiar enough, but in this book we shall argue that it is worse than useless as a way of understanding the relationship between biology and the social sciences. It is quite widely acknowledged that no organic characteristic is attributable exclusively to either nature or nurture; but what is not so commonly admitted is that the very idea of partitioning such characteristics into nature and nurture is profoundly mistaken. It is not that we must find room for both nature and nurture in the human sciences, but rather that we must abandon the very attempt to devise an algebra by which any two such entities are supposedly related in the development of behaviour.

Throughout this book we shall be arguing that the persistence of the false dichotomy between nature and nurture has been responsible for much needless conflict over animal and human aggression. Once again, this way of thinking – in all its varied forms (nature versus nurture, genes versus environment, instinct versus learning, etc.) – owes as much to the influence of wider society as it does to any technical demands arising within science. As soon as we begin to shake ourselves free from the sterile oppositions of 'common sense', however, we start to see that we are not required to choose between biology and the social sciences at all. Then, and only then, do we become free to embark upon the far more ambitious but also far more amiable task of constructing a view of human aggression that does justice to the insights to be found within both disciplines. In order to have any chance of success in this undertaking, however, we shall find it necessary continually to be on our guard against an image of the relationship between the natural world and human culture that has dominated the human sciences for generations.

Science and the social reality of aggression

The task of freeing ourselves from longstanding prejudices about nature and culture is not made any easier by the passion that is aroused by the third of our fundamental questions; namely, the relationship between the scientific study of aggression and the social reality of human conflict. Conflict and violence are quite properly of moral and political concern both to many lay people and to many behavioural scientists. As we have seen, such concern has played a large part in the growth of scientific interest in aggression. At the same time, however, it has led many behavioural scientists to disagree strongly with one another over the potential practical applications of their work. Thus, inherent in the polarized view of the relationship between biology and the social sciences which was described above, there is a disagreement that is at heart a conflict over values. It will be recalled, for example, that Rose, Kamin, and Lewontin do not criticize biological determinism only for its 'reductionism', but also for its 'reductionism in the service of the status quo'.

It is not hard either to see or to sympathize with their point of view. If to provide a biological explanation of behaviour is also to provide an account of why that behaviour is a necessary and an inevitable part of our lives (as biological determinism would have us believe), then we may well be suspicious of the very idea of going to biology for explanations of the way we behave. For on this view, biology is destiny; and who among us wishes to have their destiny dictated to them by their DNA? Equally, if to provide a social explanation of human behaviour is, by the same token, to bring that behaviour into the realm of human choice (as many of the critics of biological determinism appear to think), then we may be inclined to look for such explanations wherever we can. For on this view sociology is freedom, and who among us would not like to be free?

There is, however, a third possibility. For if, as we shall argue, the very equation of biology with destiny and sociology with freedom is profoundly mistaken, then perhaps – and at long last – we may be led to consider calmly and with a degree of objectivity what the various branches of the human sciences can teach us about ourselves. At the very least, we may be able to pursue our inquiry into human aggression without the nagging – and, on reflection, intrinsically absurd – fear that the scope for effective human action will somehow be restricted by the growth of our knowledge.

This book contains a great many criticisms of things that are often said about aggressive behaviour in the name of science. It is important to state clearly at the outset, therefore, that the book is intended as both a contribution to science and a critique of scientism – the distortion and misappropriation of science for ideological purposes. Whereas science can ennoble and enrich the human spirit, scientism can only enfeeble it. Responsibly conducted and wisely applied, it may be that scientific analysis of animal and human conflict will make a useful contribution to the efforts of well-meaning people everywhere to construct a safer and a more peaceable world. If it is to do so, however, we shall have to put firmly behind us a number of scientistic ideas that currently surround the subject of aggression. Prominent among such scientistic ideas is the myth of 'the beast within', and it is to this that we turn next.

CHAPTER TWO

The myth of the beast within

The popular conception of aggression

On 7 April 1978 a popular English newspaper (the *Daily Mail*) ran a feature article under the arresting headline 'The Startling Secret of Man'. 'Why do we love', it asked, 'why do we hate, and, most important, why do we work ...?' The article suggested that the answers to these questions were to be found in 'New Improved Super Economics ... with the new magic biological ingredient!' (Figure 2.1). According to the latest findings of biologists, it explained, the human body was simply an elaborate machine designed to preserve its genes and pass them on to its offspring. Basic to this machine's design were a number of combative and competitive instincts that were the foundations of all social life. 'Our

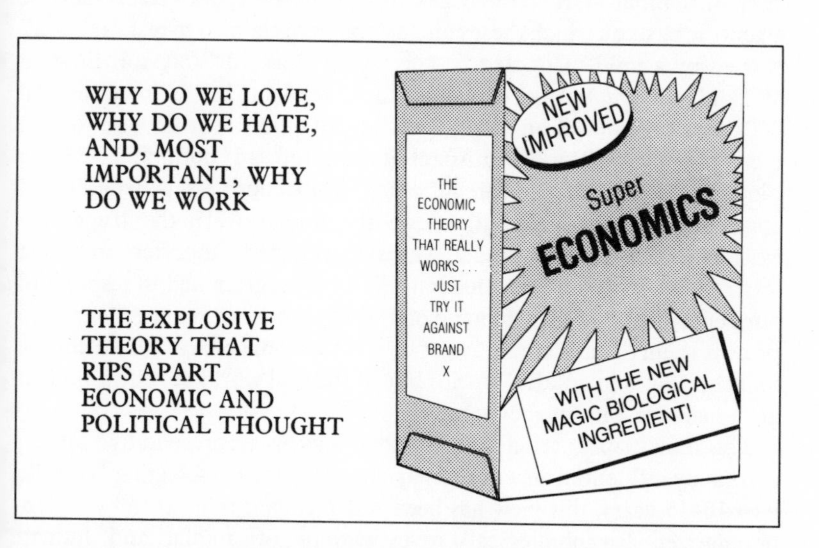

Figure 2.1 This is how the *Daily Mail* (7 April 1978) announced to its readers E.O. Wilson's recent disclosure of 'The Startling Secret of Man'. The 'new magic biological ingredient' was, of course, sociobiological theory; and the 'startling secret' was that, despite all appearances, humans were nothing but selfish gene machines.

genes', it claimed, 'needing to survive and prosper, turn man into an aggressive animal who will always seek to better himself at the expense of his peers.' Such genetic selfishness had important practical consequences. Not only did it 'foredoom to disaster' any political system that sought to reduce or remove the competitive element in human affairs, but also it endorsed any system that put a premium upon self-help. 'The Conservative case thus becomes biologically valid as the Socialist case becomes biologically invalid.' '*We are what we are*', the article declared, adding italics for greater emphasis, '*greedy, rapacious, self-serving individuals, out to get what we can for ourselves and Devil take the hindmost.*' And in case there should remain even a single reader who had somehow failed to see where the argument was leading, it concluded by stating that, 'It will be a chilling thought to many, but it does begin to look as if we have a little bit of Maggie Thatcher in us all'.

The political message of this popular article is familiar enough, and so too is the view of human nature on which it is based. The economics of self-interest is represented most famously in Adam Smith's *Wealth of Nations* (1776); and the image of human nature as fundamentally combative and competitive is portrayed most clearly in Thomas Hobbes's *Leviathan* (1651). In fact, what was new about the *Daily Mail*'s 'New Improved Super Economics' was not its conclusions – these were, and remain, standard fare in the pages of many newspapers – but rather the scientific basis on which these conclusions were claimed to rest. 'It was all started by a mild-mannered be-spectacled Harvard Professor, Edward Wilson', the *Daily Mail* explained to its readers. In his 'monumental 700-page book' (Wilson 1975), he had put 'the scientific case for the concept of original sin'. Old Adam, it appeared, was nothing less than a biological legacy of egoism, inherited from countless generations of ancestors who had fought with one another for survival in the struggle for existence. The result was that, 'We have been made imperfect and must learn to live with our imperfections. We are programmed to respond to our genes, which in turn demand of us that we behave in a specific way to protect them.' Conflict might not be what rational beings would choose for themselves in an ideal world; but in the real world of selfish human gene machines, it was inevitable.

The newspaper article on sociobiology is representative of an extremely influential view of human nature in western societies. Over the past 10–15 years, this view has been reflected and reinforced by widely popularized 'sociobiological' investigations of animal and human behaviour. As heralded by Edward Wilson in 1975, sociobiology is 'the systematic study of the biological basis of all social behavior' (Wilson 1975). To be more precise, sociobiology is the systematic study of the evolution of social behaviour; and to appreciate its true significance, we must first understand Charles Darwin and Alfred Russel Wallace's theory of evolution by natural selection.

According to the Darwinian theory, evolution occurs in reproducing populations of organisms as a result of the combined effect of several rather simple processes: first, organisms tend to pass on their characteristics to their offspring (this is Darwin's principle of inheritance, which is represented today in terms of the transmission of genes – the units of inheritance); secondly, from time to time offspring may be born with quite new characteristics, which are in turn passed on to subsequent generations (this is Darwin's principle of heritable variation, which is represented today in terms of the occurrence of random genetic mutations); and, thirdly, in any one generation there may be differences between individuals with respect to reproductive success that are directly attributable to heritable variation within the population (this is Darwin's principle of natural selection). Darwin's startling claim was that the accumulation down the generations of small heritable variations by virtue of their enhancement of the relative reproductive success of individuals within reproducing populations has been the principal engine of evolutionary change in the history of life.

Sociobiologists are Darwinians, and their job is to find out how the principle of natural selection applies to the social behaviour of animals and humans. In principle, at least, it is easy to see how natural selection may produce behaviour that promotes the relative reproductive success of the behaving individual. However, it is a striking feature of much social behaviour that it appears to lower the relative reproductive success of one individual to the direct benefit of another. It has been a central aim of sociobiologists to account for this apparent anomaly, by showing how even the most self-sacrificial social behaviour may be generated by the Darwinian mechanism. For example, by laying down their lives for close relatives, individuals may promote the survival of genes that they share with such relatives by common descent. In the metaphorical language of Richard Dawkins (1976), such 'altruistic' behaviour is described as serving the interests of an actor's 'selfish genes'.

This and related issues will be considered more fully in Chapter 3. For the moment, however, we are less concerned with the scientific content of sociobiology than with the popular imagery that has come to surround it; and here, at least, the *Daily Mail* is a useful guide. For from its very inception, sociobiology has been associated with a particular cluster of ideas about human nature. These are, first, that genes 'programme' human behaviour, in the sense that they dictate particular actions; secondly, that genetically programmed behaviour is uniformly selfish, in the sense that it promotes the individual actor's interests; and, thirdly, that genetically programmed selfishness is the foundation of much or all human economic, social, and political life, in the sense that such selfishness prescribes some forms of collective activity and proscribes others.

Taken together, these ideas present us with a view of humans as beings driven by biological forces more or less beyond their conscious control. Programmed to compete with one another for survival and reproduction, they appear to have no option but to submit to the demands of a nature whose first law is what Hobbes termed the 'war, as is of every man, against every man'.

The image of humans as the hapless victims of their selfish natures has dogged sociobiology from the very beginning. Inspired, perhaps, by Wilson's remark that 'the organism is only DNA's way of making more DNA' (Wilson 1975), and Dawkins's comment that 'Genes, unlike diamonds, are forever' (Dawkins 1976), the media have become bedazzled by the role of biology in human affairs. Thus, on 24 July 1977 the colour magazine of the *Sunday Times* newspaper in Britain presented an account of human sociobiology under the headline: 'Genes, are they really our enemies within?', followed by, 'A woman's place is in the home; man is polygamous ... a controversial new theory of genetics suggests this is the natural order of things'. Just one week later (1 August), *Time* magazine in America ran a similar story under a front cover showing two human puppet figures, male and female, gazing past one another as they dangled helplessly on their genetic strings in the gesture of a frozen embrace.

This image represents, if not what Wilson and Dawkins intended to say, at least what they were very widely taken to be saying. Indeed, Dawkins himself has described how, without his knowledge, the German and French editions of *The Selfish Gene* were published with jacket portraits of a human puppet jerking on strings labelled 'genes', and clockwork men with wind-up keys, respectively (Figure 2.2). Dawkins's comment upon these portraits is revealing: 'I have had slides of both covers made up', he writes, 'as illustrations of what I was *not* trying to say' (Dawkins 1982, p.17).

Once again, we defer consideration of the scientific misunderstandings hinted at in this last quotation in order to concentrate on the popular image of humans as selfish gene machines. This notion appeals to the twin views, deep-rooted in our culture, (1) that nature is a fixed order set over against the domain of human affairs, and (2) that this nature is an obstacle in the path of human aspirations. Overwhelmingly, popular imagery relating to human sociobiology presents a gloomy portrait of the deepest human impulses as fundamentally egocentric. This is very largely because, by a variety of manoeuvres, the genetic processes that are presumed to have been responsible for fashioning human nature are conflated with the psychological egoism that is presumed to lie at the heart of all human conduct. In this way, the evolutionary process is endowed with a moral bias towards selfishness; and we are portrayed as its victims.

Pesisimistic versions of this position incline towards fatalism, whereas optimistic versions tend to portray the human condition as a battle between an ignoble nature and a noble culture devoted to redirecting or repressing nature's worst tendencies. Either way, however, the assumption remains the same: what is natural in us is of little or no moral worth. Perhaps we must simply endure the consequences of our nasty natures, or perhaps we may somehow suppress them in some grand effort of individual or collective will; but however this may be, we can, as Richard Dawkins once put it, 'expect little help from biological nature' in our struggle to lead a worthy life. 'Let us try to *teach* generosity and altruism, because we are born selfish' (Dawkins 1976, p.3).

We have already suggested that the image of human nature contained in popularized sociobiology is not new. In fact, something very close to it has figured in many pre- and non-evolutionary philosophies of human nature in western culture. For example, compare the image we have been discussing with the familiar view of human nature that has always been a prominent strand in Christian thought on this subject. According to the doctrine of original sin, Adam's rebellion against God in the Garden of Eden marred the whole human race (if not the entire Creation). As a result of this first sinful act, humankind inherited a common nature biased permanently towards evil rather than good. To St Paul, there were two principles or laws of conduct at war with one another inside each person: the law of sin, to which all were enslaved by nature; and the law of God, to which some were delivered by grace (see, for example, *Romans* 7: 18–24). Unregenerate humankind was, quite literally, predisposed by descent towards selfishness.

The similarities between this venerable doctrine and the idea of the selfish human gene machine are striking, and they have been widely noted in both the technical and the popular literature. Writing in the London newspaper *The Times* on 17 March 1984, for example, the Christian physicist Russel Stannard argued that, 'the biblical idea of original sin ... gains a measure of support from the theory of evolution'. Enlarging on this theme elsewhere, Stannard has described how a 'self-seeking, aggressive trait, so essential to survival in the past, seems ... to be eradicably [*sic*] etched into the fabric of our bodies (in the form of the

Figure 2.2 These front covers for the French and German language editions of Richard Dawkins's *The Selfish Gene* illustrate clearly what Dawkins's editors, at least, took to be the

message of the book. For what Dawkins himself thought of this interpretation of his work, see the discussion in the text.

DNA molecules) and thereby into our mental makeup'. Given the innate aggressiveness of human nature, together with the possession of nuclear weapons, Stannard sees a dismal prospect for our species. The real question, he suggests, is not *whether* we shall use nuclear weapons to destroy ourselves completely, but rather *when* we shall do so (Stannard 1982); and all this, simply because we are presumed to be dancing to the deathly tune of our DNA.

Over and again in recent years, popular accounts of sociobiology have reverted to a secular version of the doctrine of original sin. By replacing the legendary past of the Garden of Eden with the prehistoric past of our evolutionary ancestry, these accounts reproduce the dualism of nature and grace in Christianity as the opposition between an ancient core of biological impulses and a modern overlay of cultural constraints. This transformation amounts to the replacement of one myth by another, which may be termed the myth of the beast within. The presence of this new, secular myth may be suspected wherever we find most or all of the following pairs of terms (or their functional equivalents) being used to describe the human condition:

Animal	Human
Nature	Nurture
Instinct	Learning
Gene	Environment
Selfishness	Altruism

Obviously, the above pairs of terms have resonances other than with the dualistic philosophy of human nature as an amalgam of biological base and social superstructure. However, they are all readily capable of being incorporated into the myth of the beast within. In the next section, we shall trace the pervasive influence of this myth across more than a century of debate about human nature and human aggression.

The myth in history

Thus far, we have concentrated almost exclusively upon popular rather than professional interpretations of human nature. However, the idea of the beast within has its origins as much in the work of prominent philosophers and scientists interested in the 'biological basis' of human behaviour as in the work of their popularizers. Indeed, like so many other important mythic themes in our culture, this one has its roots in classical Greek philosophy, its trunk in early Christianity, and its branches in a great diversity of modern philosophy and science. To document properly the influence of this theme over more than two millennia would thus require a comprehensive intellectual history; and this alone would require an entire book.

Clearly, a comprehensive history of this kind is impossible in the present context. Instead, we must be content with just one or two examples of the myth of the beast within from the modern period. These have been chosen to illustrate both the seriousness with which major theorists of human nature in the past century have held one or another version of the idea of the beast within, and the wide range of contexts in which they have applied it.

Before presenting these examples, however, it is important to observe that mythic themes may assume many different forms. In the present case, the idea of the beast within has at its heart the dualism between (biological) nature and (social) nurture; but the qualities and values attached to each may vary. For example, in the modern tradition stemming from the work of the seventeenth-century English philosopher Thomas Hobbes, nature is rapacious and selfish and has to be (partially) tempered by culture; whereas in another modern tradition stemming from the work of the eighteenth-century French philosopher Jean-Jacques Rousseau, nature is harmonious and cooperative and has been extensively corrupted by culture.

For two centuries, the Hobbesian and the Rousseauian traditions have coexisted in uneasy tension with one another. Significantly, elements of each are detectable in some of the examples given below. What is striking, however, is the extent to which both traditions share common presumptions rooted in a common myth of the duality of human nature. Bad beasts, not-so-bad beasts, and good beasts are all on offer; but each presumes that humanity possesses a natural legacy which is at odds with the demands of society. It is only by recognizing the enormous potential of this simple idea that we shall be able to account for the tenacious hold of the myth of the beast within upon both the public and the scientific mind, past and present.

Charles Darwin

Charles Darwin (1809–82) is rightly acknowledged to be the father of modern evolutionary theory. A comfortably wealthy and – for the last half of his life – reclusive Victorian naturalist, he wrote what is generally and rightly regarded as the single greatest work in the history of biology: the *Origin of Species* (1859). This book was largely responsible for converting a majority of professional biologists to an evolutionary view of organic origins, though it was at first much less successful in gaining acceptance for its most original contribution, the theory of natural selection. Undaunted, Darwin went on to apply this theory to humans; and in *The Descent of Man* (1871) and *The Expression of the Emotions* (1872), he set out what remains to this day the most comprehensive theoretical treatment of human evolution.

Darwin first developed and recorded his evolutionary ideas in a series of private notebooks that he kept between 1837 and 1839. Written shortly after his return from the voyage of the *Beagle*, and with that extraordinary adventure as their major inspiration, these notebooks reveal Darwin's path to a totally new perspective on the living world. Unconstrained by public opinion, Darwin set down here his emerging views on the origins of his own species – body and soul. As early as 1838, he privately regarded as proven the animal ancestry of humans; and on this basis, he began to ask searching questions about the development of the most complex qualities that distinguish us from our relatives. How had we come to possess consciousness, language, and reason; and, above all, given that we shared a common ancestry with the apes, how on earth had we come to possess a moral sense or conscience?

Darwin's sense of the importance of this last question came not only from his characteristically Victorian judgement that morality was the most important distinguishing mark of humanity, but also from his developing evolutionary theory, which made the struggle for existence the principal engine of organic change through time. During the *Beagle* voyage, Darwin had been frankly horrified by his first encounter with the uncivilized inhabitants of Tierra del Fuego. These people, whom he saw as representative of 'man in his lowest & most savage state' (Barlow 1933), appeared to be locked into a brutal and degrading struggle for existence. How, then, had humankind advanced from such a state to a condition in which the nobler sentiments of beauty and goodness were able to flourish? Darwin regarded this as a biological problem that his new theory ought to be able to tackle.

The outlines of Darwin's resolution of this difficulty are clear in the notebooks. As products of the evolutionary process, Darwin accepted that humans possessed a number of rude and selfish instincts fitting individuals for survival in the struggle for existence. But, he suggested, at a key stage in their development, primitive humans had banded together in groups for mutual protection; and at that point, natural selection had begun to favour more advanced, altruistic sentiments fitting individuals for cooperative life in society. The conflict between selfish and social instincts occurred in animals as well as in humans; but in humans alone there existed the capacity to reflect upon past conduct. In cases where the selfish had temporarily mastered the social instincts, Darwin argued that such reflection would produce feelings of dissatisfaction and regret; and in such feelings lay the origins of guilt. In a key passage, Darwin observed that the possession of powerful and barely controllable instincts 'is far from odd ... with lesser intellect they might be necessary & no doubt were preservative, & are now, like all other structures slowly vanishing ... Our Descent, then, is the origin of our evil passions!! – The Devil under form of Baboon is our grandfather!' (Gruber and Barrett 1974, p. 289).

For Darwin, then, human selfishness was the result of a legacy of anachronistic animal impulses in conflict with the demands of contemporary social life. In *The Descent of Man*, he presented this theory in the context of a generally optimistic view of the prospects for humankind. This optimism stemmed not only from his cautious support for the eugenic theories of his cousin Francis Galton (of which more below), but also from his 'Lamarckian' belief that the improving effects of habit and instruction were heritable. Following Galton, Darwin noted that 'Man ... might by selection do something not only for the bodily constitution and frame of his offspring, but for their intellectual and moral qualities'. However, he went on immediately to note that 'the moral qualities are advanced, either directly or indirectly, much more through the effects of habit, the reasoning powers, instruction, religion, &c., than through natural selection' (Darwin 1871). Either way, since for Darwin there was an archaic beast within human nature in the form of an evolutionary legacy of selfish instincts, it was only by future heritable change that real improvements in the human condition could be achieved.

Francis Galton

Francis Galton (1822–1911) was, by his own account, a Victorian genius. Having inherited a substantial fortune at the age of 22, he devoted the rest of his long life to a mixture of exploration, invention, and scientific research. His scientific interests spanned meteorology (he coined the term 'anticyclone'), biology (he performed experiments designed to test the Lamarckian hypothesis of the inheritance of acquired characteristics), psychology (he was the father of individual difference psychology and a pioneer in the study of 'nature and nurture'), and criminology (he played an important part in the development of fingerprinting). In addition to all this, Galton was the originator of what is probably the most ambitious and certainly the most controversial social philosophy ever to have been based on the systematic application of biological principles to human affairs: eugenics (for a detailed history, see Kevles 1985). The inspiration for virtually all of this scientific output (even including fingerprinting) was a distinctive view of the beastliness of human nature.

Galton had worked mainly in geography and meteorology until 1859, when the publication of his cousin's *Origin of Species* transformed his life. The book, he wrote much later, had driven away 'the constraint of my old superstition as if it had been a nightmare'. Henceforth, he devoted himself to uncovering the biological foundations of human nature. But the religious crisis provoked by Darwin's ideas left its mark on Galton's later work, as he sought a secular explanation of human imperfection and a scientific solution to human ills. In 1865, he set out the thesis that was to preoccupy him for almost half a century. In humans, he asserted, 'talent is transmitted by inheritance to a very remarkable degree' (Galton 1865). This conclusion was based upon the study of 'talented' families (Galton was impressed, for example, by the number of eminent scientists in his own family tree!) and it received more detailed treatment in his book *Hereditary Genius* (1869). But from the outset, Galton leapt from this genetic theory to the conclusion that humanity must immediately set about improving itself – making itself more talented, for example – by selective breeding.

The clue to this instant and abiding preoccupation with eugenics is contained in the conclusion to Galton's 1865 article. For having described the course of human evolution from 'savagery' to civilization, he characterized the achievements of human culture to date as 'only skin-deep'. It was a familiar idea, he noted, that 'man is born with an imperfect nature ... tainted with sin, which prevents him from doing the things he knows to be right'. In the light of evolution, however, Galton pointed out that this imperfection must be the consequence, not of a fall from an original state of perfection, but of a rapid and very recent rise from an original state of barbarism. As he put it in a later essay, humans had inherited from their barbaric ancestors a whole battery of 'base moral instincts and intellectual deficiencies' that barred the way to genuine social progress. This 'hereditary taint', therefore, must be bred out in order to secure any real advance in the face of nature (Galton 1883).

It is now clear why Galton so consistently presented eugenics as a new religion capable of securing the salvation of humankind under a scientific priesthood of genetic engineers. For eugenics rested on a philosophy of human nature that was a simple secularization of the doctrine of original sin. The core of barbaric instincts to which Galton believed his psychometric techniques gave him direct access was the same set of devilish impulses that Darwin had identified as humankind's inheritance from the world of the apes. But where Darwin believed that individual effort might alter this inheritance directly, his cousin – convinced by his own experiments that the Lamarckian doctrine was wrong – came to believe in a scientific version of the theological doctrine of predestination. For Galton, as for the Protestant theologian John Calvin, individuals were 'elected' by forces beyond their control to either salvation or damnation. No amount of individual effort could alter the beast within; only God (according to Calvin) or the stockbreeder (according to Galton) could do that. Strange as it may seem, what Thomas Huxley was to dub 'pigeonfanciers' polity' grew out of the union of Calvinism and Darwinism.

Sigmund Freud

Sigmund Freud (1856–1939) was a Viennese doctor, anatomist, and neurologist who, from about 1885, developed the theory and clinical practice of what has become known as psychoanalysis. In doing so, he contributed not merely a new method for the treatment of mental illness but also a new metaphysic for the interpretation of everyday life. More than perhaps any other philosopher or scientist in the modern period (except perhaps Karl Marx), Freud developed a way of thinking about the human condition that has spread far beyond the academic worlds of medicine and psychiatry, transforming the terms in which ordinary people make sense of their experience. For this reason, it is particularly significant that Freud's view of human nature was also a variant of the idea of the beast within.

The task of summarizing Freud's view of human nature is extremely difficult, not least because he changed his mind repeatedly on even the most basic issues. For example, in the first phase of his transition from neurology to psychology, he clearly hoped to be able to formulate a physiological model for mental processes. *The Project for a Scientific Psychology* (1885) was written in terms derived from the 'physicalist' physiology of Freud's teacher Ernst Brücke and his colleagues Hermann Helmholtz, Emile du Bois-Reymond, and Carl Ludwig. Here, Freud sought to base psychological processes on a neurone-discharge model of the central nervous system in which quantities of psychic 'energy' are imagined to accumulate and discharge in a lawful way. But he soon abandoned this quest for a neurophysiology of the mind in favour of a more strictly psychological approach. The assumption of determinism in psychic life remained, as did the notions of psychic energy and its lawful transformation in the mind; but these principles were progressively detached from any concrete physiological processes.

Just as there was a continuity in the influence of nineteenth-century neurophysiology in Freud's work, so also there was a continuity in the influence of nineteenth-century evolutionary theory. Inspired by the English neurologist John Hughlings Jackson, among others, Freud came to see the human mind as an ontogenetic (developmental) and phylogenetic (evolutionary) hierarchy of structural and functional levels. According to the then-popular doctrine of recapitulation, the individual organism was supposed to pass through the successive stages of its evolutionary history in the course of its embryological development. Freud applied this idea to the mind, arguing that in mental development individuals recapitulate the psychosexual evolution of the species. But whereas in physical ontogeny the intermediate stages were transient, in mental ontogeny Freud argued that they persist and conflict with one another. In 1919, he wrote:

> Man's archaic heritage forms the nucleus of the unconscious mind; and whatever part of that heritage has to be left behind in the advance of later phases of development, because it is unserviceable or incompatible with what is new and harmful to it, falls victim to the process of (organic) repression (Strachey 1966–74, Vol.17, pp. 203–4).

Here we see what might be termed an evolutionary theory of the unconscious, in which primitive energies inherited from the remote past well up in the mind to generate felt needs and desires, these being either satisfied in the cathartic release of appropriate activities or suppressed in the (potentially psychopathogenic) process of what Freud termed 'organic repression' (for a fuller account, see Sulloway 1979).

It is this evolutionary conception of the human mind as a core of ancient and unconscious impulses overlain by a skin of modern and (sub)conscious constraints that provides the basis for most of Freud's clinical theory (his ideas of psychosexual development, of character formation, of psychopathology, and of psychoanalytic therapy), as well as much of his metapsychology (his views on the nature of nervous and mental processes, his psychodynamics, and so forth). Above all, it is this conception that is at the heart of his views on the place of instinct in human life. In *The Ego and the Id* (1923), Freud revised his model of the mind once again so as to take account not only of the basic dualism of instinct (id) and reason (ego) but also of moral conscience (superego). Once again, however, it was in the tension between the lesser and the more evolved that he saw the basic axis of mental life. The relationship between ego and id was, he wrote, like 'a man on horseback, who has to hold in check the superior strength of the horse' (Strachey 1953–74, Vol.19, p. 25).

In his later writings, Freud came to see eros (including sex) and thanatos (including aggression) as the two most important instinctive energies. Spurred on by his own traumatic response to the horror of the First World War, he moved towards an increasingly pessimistic view of the human intellect as a 'plaything' of unconscious forces, including those 'primitive, savage and evil impulses' so awfully revealed in the trenches of Europe (Stepansky 1977). In *Civilization and its Discontents* (1930), he extended this dualistic philosophy of human nature into a theory of the inevitable conflict between the demands of instinct and those of civilization. Dismissing as an 'untenable illusion' the idea that humans are fundamentally good but corrupted by circumstance, he portrayed aggression as 'an innate, independent instinctual disposition'; and the sombre question with which he left his readers was whether and to what extent humankind would succeed in mastering the beast within.

Konrad Lorenz

Konrad Lorenz (b. 1903) is one of the founders of ethology, the branch of biology devoted to animal behaviour. Working principally with various species of birds at his home in Altenberg, Austria, in the 1930s, and after the war for many years at the Max-Planck-Institüt für Verhaltens-physiologie in Seewiesen über Starnberg, southern Germany, Lorenz championed the sympathetic study of the behaviour of animals under natural or semi-natural conditions. Having developed an ambitious theory of the instinctive basis of both animal and human behaviour, he went on to apply it to a wide range of contemporary social and political problems. Lorenz's attempt to analyse human aggression from a biological point of view has been enormously influential, and it is discussed at various points in this book. For the present, we are concerned simply to indicate that his analysis was very much a part of the intellectual tradition with which we are now concerned.

The key to all of Lorenz's theoretical work was the distinction between the innate and the learned components of behaviour. This distinction – which was greatly modified over the years, but never abandoned – rested on Lorenz's conviction that, in the course of animal evolution, behaviour had been built up in precisely the same way as anatomy. Just as natural selection had produced those physical characteristics that enable animals to survive, so, too, it had produced those behavioural characteristics that served the same end. Thus, animals came into the world equipped with such specific behavioural capacities and dispositions as they required for survival; and these provisions Lorenz termed 'innate', in order to distinguish them from responses whose origins lay wholly in the individual animal's experience.

Alongside and in close harmony with his ideas about the evolution of behaviour by natural selection, Lorenz developed a model of the causal mechanism by which innate behaviour is generated in the interaction between animals and their environments. This model consisted of accumulating reserves of instinctive energy that could be 'released' into one or more behavioural pathways by a variety of appropriate stimuli (for a more detailed discussion of this model, see Chapter 7). The virtue of this model, from Lorenz's point of view, was that by combining internal (energetic) and external (releasing) factors, it allowed for the assignment of distinct roles to innate and learned components in the genesis of adaptive behaviour. Most fundamentally important behaviour sequences, together with their specific releasing mechanisms, were innate in animals and thus relatively stereotyped in their performance – examples here would be many courtship and territorial displays; but learning could influence such details as the particular circumstances in which these displays might occur, and the particular objects at which they might be directed.

This drive model of instinct was, of course, remarkably similar to Freud's. In retrospect, Lorenz explicitly acknowledged the convergence of the psychoanalytic and his own view of instinct; and he identified as crucial to this convergence 'Freud's basic discovery ... of the central nervous system as a dualism between internal drives welling up and higher, superimposed centres repressing those drives' (Evans 1975). Like Freud also, Lorenz applied his instinct theory to human aggression and warfare. But where Freud had contrasted the life (including sex) and death (including aggression) instincts, Lorenz was deeply committed to an evolutionary perspective in which all instincts must have (or have had) definite survival value. In his best-selling work *On Aggression* (1966) – significantly entitled *Das Sogenannte Böse* (The so-called evil) in the original German – Lorenz therefore set out to establish the survival value of innate aggression in animals, as a prelude to diagnosing what had gone so disastrously wrong in humans.

Lorenz's position was as follows. In animals in the wild, he suggested, carefully regulated release of aggressive energy served many purposes, from the spacing out of members of a species over the available territory, to ensuring that only the fittest individuals reproduced. In each case, the potential for inflicting damage was carefully controlled so as to prevent animals from behaving in ways harmful to the survival of their species. In humans alone, however, the inception of cultural evolution – and particularly the discovery of weapons – had upset the delicate balance of nature. For now, the rapidly advancing capacity to inflict harm soon rendered totally inadequate the innate controls on aggression. Hence Lorenz's diagnosis (1966, p. 40):

> An unprejudiced observer from another planet, looking upon man as he is today, in his hand the atom bomb, the product of his intelligence, in his heart the aggression drive inherited from his anthropoid ancestors, which this same intelligence cannot control, would not prophesy long life for the species.

Lorenz's ethological analysis of the human condition was a romantic and Rousseauian version of the idea of the beast within. For just as Rousseau had described the history of humankind as the passage from 'noble savagery' to ignoble civilization, so Lorenz portrayed the forest home of our primate ancestors as a Garden of Eden that had become Paradise Lost when the hominids moved out onto the savannah plains. There was much truth, he wrote, in the Biblical 'parable of the tree of knowledge and its fruit'. For it was knowledge – born of conceptual thought, language, and the explosive growth of culture – that had 'robbed man of the security provided by his well-adapted instincts' (Lorenz 1966). For Lorenz, humans were uniquely out of step with their own aggressive natures, and thus uniquely at risk of causing their own – and everybody else's – demise. His recommended solutions to this dilemma were the pursuit of greater self-knowledge, and the quest for new and harmless channels along which to discharge our aggression. Above all, Lorenz warned in the metaphor used earlier by Freud that, 'Man must know that the horse he is riding may be wild and should be bridled' (Evans 1974; see also Evans 1975).

Paul MacLean

Paul D. MacLean (b.1913) is an American neuroanatomist and psychiatrist, and the chief exponent of the best-known general model of vertebrate brain/behaviour evolution in the post-war period. Beginning in the late 1940s at the Massachusetts General Hospital in collaborative work with the psychiatrist Stanley Cobb, and later at Yale University, where he worked with the neurophysiologist John Fulton, and at the National Institute of Mental Health in Bethesda, Maryland, where in 1971 he was appointed Chief of the Laboratory of Brain Evolution and Behavior, MacLean has built up a substantial programme of research around his doctrine of the 'triune brain' (MacLean 1973). Briefly, this is the doctrine that humans possess three structurally and functionally distinct brains in one. Arranged rather like the successive layers of an onion (see Figure 2.3), these distinct brains embody the successive stages of higher vertebrate behavioural evolution. The oldest, 'reptilian' brain houses the most basic instincts; the next, 'palaeomammalian' brain looks

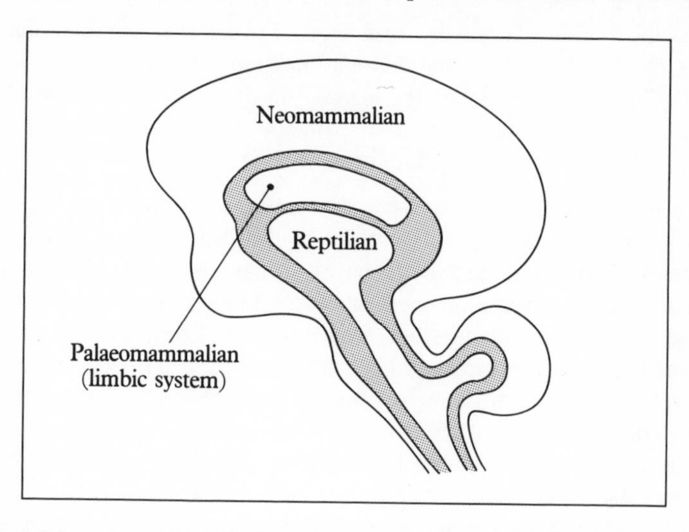

Figure 2.3 According to Paul MacLean, the evolution of the brain occurred as a series of surges or waves with succeeding levels superimposed on more-or-less unchanged existing structures.

after the more complex emotions; and the youngest, 'neomammalian' brain is responsible for the most elevated attributes of the human mind. Thus, MacLean considers that we are beings 'under the joint direction of three different mentalities' (MacLean 1982).

The origins of the doctrine of the triune brain are to be found in almost a century of research based on the twin principles of functional localization within the nervous system and the hierarchical organization of nervous structures and functions within an evolutionary series (for further details, see Durant 1985). On this view, not only are specific aspects of behaviour controlled by specific regions of the brain, but successive stages in the evolution of brain and behaviour are preserved intact within the nervous systems of the higher vertebrates. As MacLean has put it, 'Nature, despite all her progressiveness, is also a staunch conservative and is more tenacious than the curator of a museum in holding on to her antiques' (MacLean 1973). In this case, 'Nature's antiques' are those primitive instincts and emotions presumed to constitute the necessary first stages in the evolution of animal behaviour. For MacLean, fixed and stereotyped behaviour, including the aggressive displays of many lower vertebrates, is a necessary preliminary to the appearance of more flexible capabilities, such as the feeling- and emotion-based interactions between mammalian parents and offspring; and these in turn are a necessary preliminary to the development of the most flexible of all capabilities, including those intelligent, language-based operations that are unique to human culture.

Clearly, MacLean's model is yet another variation on the theme of the beast within. On this occasion, things are complicated by the fact that there are three distinct levels involved rather than the more usual two. But this does not affect the central theme, which is that humans are the victims of a battle between opposing natural and cultural elements in their makeup. Over the years, MacLean has used the alleged conflict between the reptilian and palaeomammalian brains, on the one hand, and the neomammalian brain, on the other, to account for everything from paranoia to mob violence and warfare. There are, he argues, 'demons' within our brains; and these demons are under only very limited and partially effective control by the conscious and rational parts of our minds (Koestler and Smythies 1972). Possessed of such a 'schizophysiology', therefore, we depend for our very survival as a species upon an improved understanding of the triune brain.

The myth in contemporary science and society

Darwin, Galton, Freud, Lorenz, and MacLean are representatives of a tradition of thought regarding the biological foundations of human nature that spans more than a century. With the work of Lorenz and MacLean, of course, we are only a short step from the contemporary scene. Throughout the 1960s and into the early 1970s, attempts to apply evolutionary theory to human behaviour were heavily influenced by ideas coming out of Lorenzian ethology. Generally, humans were presumed to be far more aggressive and violent towards one another than were the members of any other species. With their stone-age instincts and space-age technologies, they were widely seen as being burdened with what the psychiatrist David Hamburg termed a 'carry-over problem' (Lee and DeVore 1972). Of course, this professional concern to define and, if possible, to domesticate the beast within caught the imaginations of popularizers and pundits; and in the work of writers such as Robert Ardrey (1961, 1966) and Arthur Koestler (1967), a generally gloomy message regarding the evolutionary origins of human sinfulness reached a wide audience. As Mary Long put it in her dramatically illustrated account of MacLean's ideas for one of the glossy science magazines, 'Deep inside your brain there exists a small but powerful primeval center every bit as violent and reptilian in nature as the brain of a lizard or crocodile' (Long 1980; see Figure 2.3).

In recent years, ethology has been transformed by new developments in evolutionary theory. Under the banner of sociobiology, older and often rather sloppy ways of applying the theory of natural selection to behaviour have given way to newer and generally more rigorous treatments inspired by the theoretical work of such men as William D. Hamilton (1964, 1971, 1972), John Maynard Smith (1964, 1965), and George C. Williams (1966). Increasingly since 1970, biologists have abandoned what they tend to see as the woolly and rather romantic ideas of the Lorenzians in favour of more disciplined and explicitly tough-minded attitudes towards animal behaviour. These attitudes are based on the assumption that natural selection acts exclusively on individual organisms, rather than on social groups or whole species. From this, it follows that, to the extent that it is the product of selection, behaviour should be 'selfish'; that is, it should serve the genetic interests of individuals, rather than those of social groups or whole species.

Once again, it is tempting to see the influence of wider society in this dramatic shift of emphasis and tone in the work of so many biologists. After all, the 1960s and early 1970s was a generally expansive period – a period in which 'romantic' talk of togetherness, of the banning of war, and of the power of love (or even of flowers) was positively fashionable; whereas by contrast the late 1970s and early 1980s was a generally more restrictive period – a period in which widespread economic recession saw a renaissance of individualism in the emergence of the 'me generation' and the replacement of 'hippies' by 'yuppies'. Superficially, at least, what was happening in biology through this period looks very like a scientific version of wider cultural changes.

Whatever its origins, the change of outlook in biology over the past 15 years has revolutionized the scientific study of aggressive behaviour. For instead of being seen (*pace* Lorenz) as a species-preserving 'instinct' inherited intact throughout whole classes or even entire phyla of animals, aggression has come to be regarded as a genetically 'selfish' tactic used flexibly by some animals, depending upon what others are doing or are likely to do. Unlike many classical ethologists, sociobiologists positively expect animals to be aggressive towards other members of their species, but only in situations where by doing so they can improve their own or their close relatives' reproductive success. At the same time, however, sociobiologists have come to have great respect for the subtlety of the relationship between behaviour and reproductive success; they do not presume, for example, that pure thuggery always pays the best dividends.

A much fuller account of these issues is provided in Chapter 8. For the present, however, the really important point is simply that sociobiology has effected a sea change in the way biologists think about behaviour. To the classical ethologists, animals appeared almost as if they were simple, self-winding mechanical toys, capable of executing only a limited number of specific tricks in response to a limited array of stereotyped triggering stimuli. But to the sociobiologists, these same animals appear rather as shrewd, scheming harlequins, capable of almost machiavellian intrigues as they plot the behavioural strategies that will best promote their selfish genetic interests. It is, of course, vital to be clear about the fact that sociobiology does not require animals actually to devise their own behaviour in this fashion; but it does require natural selection to be capable of generating behavioural strategies of such subtlety and sophistication that sociobiologists are often obliged to think like scheming harlequins themselves in order to understand what animals are really up to!

It is not difficult to see why, in some quarters, sociobiology has been appropriated as a new source of scientific support for the doctrine of original sin. Even more than some of the classical ethologists, with their romantic ideas about animals restraining themselves in the larger interests of the species, some sociobiologists (and rather more of their admirers, both in other academic disciplines and in the media) have seen in evolutionary social theory the true foundation for a fundamentally Hobbesian philosophy of human nature.

To illustrate the argument involved here, consider just one comparatively sophisticated recent attempt to apply sociobiology to the human condition. In 1975, the psychologist Donald Campbell chose as the theme for his presidential address before the American Psychological Association 'the conflict between biological and social evolution and between psychology and moral tradition'. On the basis of sociobiological reasoning, Campbell urged his colleagues to consider the possible functions of traditional religious moralizing. The portrait of a 'biologically based social personality' that was emerging from sociobiology, he informed them, was one of 'predominantly self-serving opportunism even for the most social species'. By nature, therefore, humans must be selfish; and it followed that all of the very considerable quantities of cooperativeness and altruism necessary to the maintenance of their complex societies must be maintained by a process of social evolution opposed at every point to the tendencies of biology. Accepting the charge that he was reviving the doctrine of original sin, Campbell invited his colleagues to see in traditional belief systems a set of cultural rules designed to resist the fundamental beastliness of human nature (Campbell 1975).

Throughout this chapter, the idea of the beast within has been referred to as a 'myth', and the time has now come to make explicit what is meant by this. There are at least two distinct but related things that may be conveyed in the claim that a particular proposition is a myth: first, that the proposition is, literally speaking, false; and secondly, that it is its metaphorical and moral (rather than literal or scientific) significance that gives it credibility within a particular society. It is in both of these senses that the label 'myth' is customarily applied to religious propositions; and it is in both of these senses that we intend it to apply to the (pseudoscientific) idea of the beast within.

Literally speaking, the idea of the beast within is at best a crudely distorted rendering of the conclusions of evolutionary biology; at worst, it is just plain wrong. This, at any rate, is what will be argued in Chapter 3. But metaphorically and morally speaking, it is clear that the idea has a persistent appeal in our society; and the reason is not hard to find. Taking its terms of reference (but, as will emerge later, precious little else) from evolutionary biology, the myth of the beast within sets up a symbolic conflict between the natural and the cultural, which, on even the most cursory inspection, turns out to embody a set of very basic concerns about good and evil; concerns which, of course, it has been the traditional role of religion to organize and articulate.

In a largely secular age, there is an obvious temptation to appeal to science instead of to religion for guidance on matters moral and social. This, however, is a temptation we should strive to resist. For inevitably, the result of giving in to it is that the distinction between science and sentiment becomes blurred; and with this blurring, there generally follows a wholesale abandonment of precisely those virtues of the scientific enterprise – factual and theoretical rigour, for example, as well as scholarly self-discipline – that are most needed if we are to have any real chance of arriving at a reasonably accurate and objective view of the human condition. The true scale of this problem in the present case can be judged only from a consideration of how far below the standards of accuracy and objectivity the myth of the beast within actually falls, and it is to this that we turn next.

CHAPTER THREE

Towards a de-mythologized biology of behaviour

Introduction

During its long history, the myth of the beast within has changed many times, taking first one and then another form in the hands of the numerous anthropologists, biologists, psychologists, sociologists, and others who have incorporated it in their writings. From the point of view of the critic, this makes it rather like the ducks on a shooting range at a funfair - no sooner has one been shot down successfully than another pops up. To win a prize in this sort of game, a player must be persistent, skillful, and vigilant; and this, as all funfair managers know, is far from easy.

For this among other reasons, we shall not criticize individually each version of the myth of the beast within that was reviewed in the previous chapter. Instead, we shall examine the major assumptions underlying all of them. By demonstrating that these assumptions are at best misleading and at worst completely false, we shall discover a number of fundamental weaknesses that must be shared by any particular version of the myth. On this basis, we shall suggest that an adequate biology of animal and human aggression depends crucially upon our willingness to de-mythologize the biological analysis of behaviour.

There are three basic assumptions underlying the myth of the beast within. These are, first, that human behaviour is a combination of the separate contributions of human nature and human culture; secondly, that human nature is necessary (i.e., it could not be other than it is), whereas human culture is contingent (i.e., it could be other than it is); and, thirdly, that human nature is fundamentally competitive and combative, whereas human culture may favour greater or lesser amounts of concord and cooperation, depending on the circumstances. These assumptions are basic in the sense that without any one of them the myth of the beast within loses all coherence. Only if they are true, for example, is it possible to give any rational meaning to the popular-scientific image of the 'selfish' human gene machine. Yet remarkably, none of these assumptions has any legitimate place within modern biology generally, or contemporary sociobiology in particular. We shall deal with each one in turn.

On human nature

First, then, we have to consider the idea that human behaviour results from the combined contributions of two discrete components: human nature and human culture. This notion crops up time and again throughout the history of Western thought, but it is strikingly exemplified in the myth of the beast within. As we have seen, the myth portrays humans as a combination of fixed natural properties and fluctuating cultural influences. Contained in this way of thinking is the notion that the natural is distinct from and prior to the cultural; the natural is somehow the core of our being, whereas the cultural is little more than an overlay of mere contingencies of time and place – rather like the veneer that conceals the rougher, structural wood beneath.

What is this thing called human nature?

If we are to think sensibly about this notion, we must first be absolutely clear about what we mean by human nature and human culture. Typically, nature and culture are defined in contrast to one another. For example, nature is commonly taken to mean the material world and its objects as opposed to the world of human civilization (as, for example, in the phrase 'nature study'); or it may mean the fundamental as opposed to the superficial properties of a thing (as, for example, in the phrase 'the nature of gold'). By the same token, human nature is commonly taken to mean what we are without the refinements of civilization (as in the phrase 'man in a state of nature'); or it may mean those essential characteristics without which we would not be ourselves at all (as in the eighteenth-century writer Richard Steele's remark that 'Men may change their climate, but they cannot their Nature').

Although this way of thinking may appear perfectly sensible, it is of little scientific use as it stands. To make more headway, we must be much more specific about what we mean. The trouble is that when we try to do this, we soon discover that there are several different possibilities. By human nature, for example, we might mean: (1) those things that only humans do (such as talking), as opposed to those that many animal species do (such as vocalizing); (2) those things that all humans do (such as smiling), as opposed to those that some do and some do not (such as cleaning their teeth); or (3) those things that all humans do without special training (such as walking), as opposed to those that they do only after such training (such as executing perfect somersaults). We shall refer to these three different notions as distinctive human nature, universal human nature, and spontaneous human nature, respectively.

Each of these notions has a certain legitimacy. If we are interested in comparing ourselves with other species, for example, we may find it useful to identify those behavioural attributes that are uniquely human. Thus, the fact that all normal adult humans talk, whereas no chimpanzees ever do so, is surely worth noting; and one way of noting it is by saying that humans have a natural ability to talk, which chimps (and all other species, so far as we know) lack. Alternatively, we may be interested in comparing ourselves with other people living in different cultures. It may be, for example, that wherever we look we find people smiling when they meet one another, more or less as we do, whereas the same is not true of shaking hands; and this time, we may say that smiling is a natural form of greeting in humans, whereas shaking hands is not. Finally, we may be interested in comparing individuals in different learning situations. Having discovered that humans are capable of walking without any special training, but that they only execute passable somersaults after considerable amounts of it, we may conclude that walking is a natural human ability, whereas somersaulting is not.

Although these three meanings of human nature are logically quite distinct, they often overlap in practice. Thus, talking is part of both our distinctive and our universal human nature, smiling is part of our universal and our spontaneous human nature, and walking (at least in the rather odd way that we do it) is part of our distinctive, our universal, and our spontaneous human nature. This alone points to the need for extreme care in the use of terms; but there is more to be said. For although talking, smiling, and walking are all natural, they are all cultural as well. After all, no one talks without acquiring a language from others during early childhood; no one smiles without engaging in progressively more complex social interactions with others; and no one walks without trial and error experience in the control and coordination of body movement. In short, talking, smiling, and walking are not only in their different ways natural but they are also in their different ways developed within cultures.

In addition to the three definitions of human nature that have now been considered, there is another closely related but slightly more sophisticated one that has especial significance for our subject. According to this definition, human nature comprises all those behavioural activities and dispositions that constitute evolved adaptations. By an evolved adaptation in this context, we mean any feature of an organism that exists because in the past natural selection favoured it over other alternatives. This definition is intended to exclude features whose existence is the indirect result of natural selection having favoured some other characteristic to which they just happen to have been linked.

At first sight, it may seem that the idea of human nature as the sum of our evolved behavioural adaptations is the same as the idea of universal human nature, which has already been discussed. In reality, however, the two conceptions are quite distinct. Thus, for example, it is at least plausible that all humans (and especially all human infants) have a tendency to like and eat chocolate if given the chance; but nobody can really suppose that this tendency was itself ever subject to the influence of evolution by natural selection. Rather more plausible, however, is the idea that something else – a tendency to like and eat sugary fruits, for example – was selected, with the predictable result that, under the altered conditions of a chocolate-manufacturing culture, parents would experience regular difficulty in restraining their children's highly developed taste for sweet things.

This example illustrates three points. First, to discover anything about human nature, where this is conceived as the sum of our evolved behavioural adaptations, we require to know which among the multitudinous things we do represent behavioural functions that were selected for among our ancestors, and which represent what might be termed behavioural effects that result from our living under conditions very different from those in which we evolved. The task of classifying human behaviour in this way is not easy, and it represents a major limitation to which any study of human behavioural evolution is inevitably subject (Symons 1979).

The second point to emerge from our example is that human nature conceived in evolutionary terms is also culture-dependent – that is, it constitutes a set of behavioural activities or dispositions that are defined in terms of what a person may be expected to do under specified circumstances; change the circumstances and, as with our example, behaviour may change accordingly. Moreover, it may not always change in ways either as predictable or as straightforward as children turning their attentions from ripe fruit on trees to chocolate in sweet-shops. We humans spend a great deal of our time doing a multitude of the most extraordinary things – from playing tunes on bassoons to putting ships into bottles – most of which it would be quite absurd to regard as evolved adaptations. Presumably, however, all of these things could be understood (if only we knew enough) in exactly the same sort of way as children's fondness for chocolate; all of them are what culture has made, and continually remakes, out of our evolved behavioural adaptations.

Thirdly, the conclusion that a particular behavioural activity or disposition is an evolved adaptation carries no implications concerning the particular roles of genes and environment in the development of that activity or disposition, save for the simple fact that such roles they must have. A lioness defending her young is almost certainly displaying an evolved adaptation, whereas a lioness jumping through a flaming hoop at a circus is not; but it is quite possible that learning enters into the first behaviour just as much as it does into the second. This is an important point, and one to which we shall return; for all too often variants on the theme of the beast within return to the contrast between the evolved and the unevolved components in behaviour on the false assumption that the former must be somehow inbuilt or 'hard-wired', whereas the latter are, so to speak, mere environmental afterthoughts. The fact is, though, that natural selection acts on all aspects of behaviour, including developmental and learning processes; and decisions about whether or not some particular activity is an evolved function are quite separate from decisions about how that activity is brought about in any given situation.

We have now considered several different meanings of the phrase 'human nature'. Doubtless, we could have considered several more; but hopefully our general point is becoming clear. Under none of the definitions we have given does the quest for a better understanding of human nature justify the use of a blanket distinction between human nature and human culture, where these are understood as the discrete and separable contributions of biological and social influences to human behaviour. Yet this blanket distinction is precisely what is embodied in so many versions of the myth of the beast within. The single most striking feature of this myth is its radically dualistic view of the human condition. That the categories of nature and culture might be ambiguous, artificial, or of strictly limited application has rarely troubled its most prominent champions; and all too often the result has been that the mere impression of scientific rigour has concealed the reality of half-baked and frankly muddled generalizations about the human condition. Where this may be understandable in the writings of early workers, it is harder to forgive now that both the biological and the human sciences have reached states of relative maturity.

On being burdened with a nature

The second key assumption underlying the myth of the beast within is that human nature is irrevocably fixed, whereas human culture is flexible. Consistently, both the major protagonists of the idea of the beast within and the major critics of it return to the notion that what is at stake between them is the question of whether or not there are natural bounds or constraints upon human liberty. On the first page of his Pulitzer Prize-winning book *On Human Nature*, Edward Wilson writes that 'we are biological and our souls cannot fly free' (Wilson 1978); and the subtitle of Melvin Konner's popular essay on human sociobiology is *Biological Constraints on the Human Spirit* (Konner 1982). Similarly, in their trenchant critique of these and similar approaches to human affairs, Steven Rose et al. tell us that, 'To the biological determinists the old credo "You can't change human nature" is the alpha and omega of the explanation of the human condition' (Rose, Lewontin, and Kamin 1984). The real problem with human nature, it would appear, is that we are stuck with it.

What sense does this make? Is it correct to say that human nature is a constraint upon human conduct in ways that human culture is not? Well, given what has gone before, it is clear that the first answer to this question must be: 'It all depends what you mean by . . .'. For example, if we take human nature to be that which makes people human, as opposed to some other kind of animal, then it is obviously true to say that, leaving aside the melodramatic sci-fi possibilities of genetic engineering, human nature is essentially fixed. People are not free to be any sorts of creatures they choose; and if there are those who would rather be chimpanzees, or chickens, or chick-peas, then clearly their liberty is to this extent restricted by their natures. It is difficult to work up very much sympathy for the plight of such people.

It is simply incredible that our inability to swap our human for some other nature lies at the root of the persistent and persistently controversial claim that 'You can't change human nature'. Rather, what appears to underlie this claim is the idea that the behavioural traits that are natural in us (in one or other of the senses considered above) are resistant to modification in a way in which others are not. This claim at least has the great advantage of not being absurd – it could be true; and if it were true, it would matter – but unfortunately, it suffers from the even greater disadvantage of being wrong. On the one hand, many behavioural responses and tendencies that develop naturally within us are open to great modification both during and long after development (think, for example, of the diverse effects of elocution lessons upon children's talking, of etiquette lessons upon their smiling, and of exercise (or injury) upon their walking). On the other hand, many behavioural responses and tendencies that are clearly not natural are extraordinarily difficult to modify by even the most ingenious means (think, for example, of the problems we encounter in 'unlearning' our own cultural codes and conventions when travelling in foreign countries; or of the sheer durability of many political and religious beliefs).

The common sense notion that 'you can't change human nature' often rests upon the largely unconscious assumption that, since human nature is biological, and more particularly genetic, it is essentially fixed at birth. In a sense (mutation and genetic engineering aside), this is true; but the fixity of genes is not at all the same thing as the fixity of their behavioural effects. As Richard Dawkins (1982) has so clearly argued, there is nothing about genetic causes of behaviour that makes them any more or less open to modification by environmental manipulation than are other causes of a more mundane kind.

There are known genetic causes of undesirable behavioural effects about which, in our present state of knowledge, we can do little (for example, Down's syndrome, one form of which is caused by the presence of an extra chromosome); and there are others about which we can do a great deal (for example, phenylketonurea, whose normally very severe symptoms may be avoided by providing a diet free from the amino acid phenylalanine). Similarly, there are known environmental causes of undesirable behavioural effects about which, in our present state of knowledge, we can do little (for example, lead poisoning in children); and there are others about which we can do a great deal (for example, many kinds of drug abuse). The point here is that the distinction gene/environment with respect to the causation of behaviour does not map onto the distinction fixed/alterable in any way whatever.

The plain fact is, then, that 'natural' traits are not by this token any more or less open to modification than are 'cultural' traits. This, on the face of it, amounts to a simple and straightforward refutation of the claim that human nature (in any of the senses in which we have defined it) is fixed in ways that human culture is not; but if this claim is so obviously wrong, why is it so often made – why, in short, is human nature so often regarded as a burden upon us? There are several possible answers to this question, including our tendency to attribute to our natures things about ourselves that we fear or dislike rather than things that please us or make us proud. In part, no doubt, this is due to a certain ('natural'?!) conceit that inclines us to take credit for our virtues while looking for someone or something else to blame for our vices; but in part, also (and these things are surely connected), it is due to a certain prejudice that leads us continually to see nature itself in human and moral terms. It is to this latter problem that we turn next.

Selfish genes or selfish beasts?

The myth of the beast within has never amounted simply to the idea that humans possess a core of natural and unalterable behavioural dispositions. Rather, it has always involved additional (though widely varying) claims about what these dispositions are like. Historically, the most popular and influential of these claims has it that at least a substantial proportion of our natural dispositions are, in old-fashioned terms, 'sinful'. (It may appear odd to describe as 'sinful' behavioural dispositions over which actors have no voluntary control; but it is worth noting that this is perfectly consistent with at least the Calvinist tradition of Protestant theology, which places great emphasis on the notion of 'predestination' to good or evil.) As popular sociobiology would have it, we are not merely 'gene machines', but 'selfish gene machines'. Impressed by sociobiology's tough-mindedly individualist attitude towards behaviour, many writers have used it to strip off what they see as the attractive veneer of kindliness and consideration on the surface of human relationships in order to reveal the far less appealing structure of aggression and conflict beneath. 'Scratch an "altruist"', as Michael Ghiselin put it in the last sentence of his book *The Economy of Nature and the Evolution of Sex* (1974), 'and watch a "hypocrite" bleed.'

The idea of human nature as fundamentally egotistical is the final ingredient in the rather unsavoury mixture of popular science and political sentiment that has been served up in the media over the past few years as an explanation of human conflict. It was because of the presumed selfishness of human nature, it will be recalled, that the *Daily Mail* saw each individual human being as 'an aggressive animal who will always seek to better himself at the expense of his peers'. On this view, selfish genes make for selfish humans, and selfish humans make for cutthroat, dog-eat-dog societies, such as the ones that appear to find favour with the editor of the *Daily Mail*.

This kind of interpretation rests on the very considerable degree of confusion that has come to surround the idea of genetic selfishness. Richard Dawkins's extended metaphor of *The Selfish Gene* (1976) was designed to convey in easily graspable, non-technical terms the fundamental logic of modern Darwinian evolutionary theory. This logic can be summarized as follows: (1) all organisms possess genes, the units of inheritance; (2) variant forms of the same gene may arise within interbreeding populations, and such variants may be responsible for bodily or behavioural differences between individual organisms; and (3) any genetic variant whose effects on the individual in which it resides are such as to promote that individual's relative reproductive success (more strictly, its 'inclusive fitness'; see Chapter 7) will increase in frequency in the population, and this is what we mean by natural selection.

Now even in summary, such conventional Darwinian logic is, to say the least of it, rather long-winded and inelegant. Richard Dawkins's great contribution was to simplify and dramatize this logic by pointing out that any evolutionarily successful gene (such as more or less any gene that has survived up to the present in a successful lineage of organisms) may be expected to possess one quality above all others, namely metaphorical 'selfishness', by which it is meant that the gene should tend to cause the individual in which it resides to behave in ways favouring that gene's continued existence.

This reformulation has the twin advantages of being a great deal easier on the ear and a great deal more convenient, particularly in connection with the analysis of certain kinds of social behaviour (Dawkins 1982). However, it has the serious disadvantage of depending upon an entirely novel usage of the word selfish. For in the opinion of Dawkins and his more discerning readers, genes are 'selfish' neither because they are inspired by selfish motives nor because they necessarily cause the organisms in which they reside to do any of the things ordinarily associated with selfish conduct; they are 'selfish' only in the totally idiosyncratic but technically precise sense that their effects on the organisms in which they reside are such as to promote their own rather than some other entity's survival through reproduction.

It is vital to be clear about the fact that such genetic 'selfishness' carries no direct implications of any kind for individual selfishness. For example, among close relatives genetic 'selfishness' may promote either fierce competition or extreme self-sacrifice, depending on the circumstances; and even among non-relatives, in repeated social interactions genetic 'selfishness' may favour anything from stable conflict to stable cooperation. It is precisely the extraordinary diversity of the behavioural outcomes that may be produced by a single evolutionary mechanism operating in a great variety of contexts that makes contemporary sociobiology such a fascinating subject. Surprising as it may seem to those well-versed in the popular literature, this very diversity demonstrates that individual selfishness possesses no particular warrant in the evolutionary process.

Some sensible biological questions

We have now exposed the most serious weaknesses of the foundations upon which the myth of the beast within rests. Given what has been said, it is clear that we need some other basis upon which to construct a scientifically and politically sensible view of animal and human aggression. This, however, is easier said than done. For what emerges from our critique is that beneath the myth of the beast within there lies a heterogeneous rubble of confused and confusing ideas about the 'biological basis' of animal and human behaviour. Before moving on, therefore, we shall spend a little time considering what might legitimately be learnt from a more sensible, de-mythologized biology of aggressive behaviour.

The Nobel Prize-winning ethologist Niko Tinbergen is well known for having distinguished between what are sometimes referred to as the 'four whys' of animal behaviour study. These are four different kinds of question having to do, respectively, with: causation, or mechanisms; survival value, or functions; evolution, or history; and ontogeny, or development (Tinbergen 1963). These questions are logically and biologically distinct, but they are interconnected in often quite subtle ways that give us some hints about the relationships between different kinds of inquiry. In this section we shall briefly discuss each 'why' with reference to aggressive behaviour, indicating not only what is but also what is not being asked under each heading.

Mechanism

What is the question?

Asking questions about causal mechanisms fits most people's idea of what biology is about. Interest in mechanism is interest in how something works. If we are interested in how a car works, we shall ask about such things as engines, gearboxes, and drive shafts. If we are interested in how an organism works, we shall ask about such things as cells, tissues, organs, and organ systems. If we are interested in how an animal's behaviour works, then we shall find ourselves discussing the brain, its sensory and motor systems, and the internal and external cues by which it orchestrates its various activities.

We shall discuss likely mechanisms of aggression in Chapter 7, but it is only fair to point out here that no completely satisfactory causal analysis of animal and human aggression is available to us at present. This is hardly surprising. Even the apparently simplest behaviour in which we are interested may require really quite sophisticated mechanisms; and even apparently identical behaviour in closely related species may work in very different ways. Full knowledge of how a given aggressive act occurs would require a more-or-less complete understanding of the nervous and muscular systems, together with a sophisticated grasp of the history of those systems in the individual organism; it hardly needs to be said that neither of these desiderata is easy to come by.

So daunting is the task of discovering mechanisms that scientists are obliged to approach it in several different and often very indirect ways. The analogy with the problem of understanding how a car works is helpful here. In principle, everything a car does could be explained in terms of the individually manufactured components that make it up; but these components are very numerous, their interconnections are very complex, and the relationships between their separate properties and the higher-level functions in which we are probably more interested (such as acceleration, deceleration, changing gear, etc.) are very remote. Of greater assistance to a novice car mechanic, therefore, would be either a 'top–down' approach, in which whole assemblies of components (engine, clutch, gearbox, etc.) were dealt with or – even more useful, perhaps – an abstract 'systems' approach, in which the car was described in terms of its major functional subsystems (fuel supply, ignition, drive, etc.).

Exactly the same principle applies in the causal analysis of aggressive behaviour. Far from representing mutually exclusive approaches, physiological, psychological, and even sociological analyses are often complementary ways of getting to grips with exceedingly complex phenomena. A particular behavioural activity may be treatable biologically in terms of receptors, analysers, and effectors, psychologically in terms of stimuli and responses, or beliefs and values, and sociologically in terms of past and present patterns of social interaction. Each level of analysis may contribute something worthwhile to our understanding of the same behaviour, just as knowledge of spark plugs, engines, and drive systems may all be useful to the would-be car mechanic. The task of putting together as complete a picture of aggression as a good mechanic has of a car is monumental; but we are less likely to make progress with it if we assume that the causal pie must be carved up into separate pieces to be doled out to biology, psychology, and the social sciences, with a bigger piece for the one meaning a smaller piece for the other.

What isn't the question?

Mechanisms have a feeling of concreteness and solidity about them; to many people they seem real, in a way that functions, evolution, and development do not. Perhaps this accounts for a certain tendency to think that this kind of causal explanation is the only really important sort of explanation in biology, and for the supposition that providing such an explanation makes a phenomenon more 'basic' or permanent than others for which no mechanism is currently known. Obviously, this is an absurd point of view. Everything a person does – digesting, fighting, playing the bassoon – depends upon discoverable mechanisms within the human body; or at least, so we shall assume. However, discovering these mechanisms for any particular behavioural activity does not make that activity any more or less biological, psychological, or social than it was before.

This is indeed obvious, but somehow it is often overlooked. In the past, for example, neurobiological investigations revealing that electrical stimulation of particular brain regions activates or inhibits certain kinds of aggressive behaviour have been taken to mean that, since such aggression is 'really' biological, or even 'pathological', the appropriate remedies for it must be physical and/or chemical (Delgado 1969; Mark and Ervin 1970). This simply does not follow. If we find a group of nerve cells whose stimulation produces anger or aggression, we have not necessarily found the place where these things are 'really' located, let alone the place that must be evacuated or even demolished if we are to live more peacefully; what we have found is a piece in a puzzle. At a neurobiological level, that puzzle may well include many other brain regions, and at a psychological and a social level it may well include processes and interactions which we would be both foolish and irresponsible to ignore.

Knowing that without spark plugs our car won't start in the morning is no substitute for knowing either how cars really work or how they may be driven safely to work. The real challenge in the study of behavioural mechanisms is to fit the individual pieces coming out of the different branches of behaviour science into the larger picture in which people act out their lives. The ultimate aim is to know how the whole system of human beings in society works at each of the levels that are appropriate to its analysis.

Function

What is the question?

Understanding of mechanisms often depends upon, or reveals the need for, an understanding of functions. The function of a thing is simply the purpose for which it exists. Many things have no function, of course. The Sun, the Earth, and the Himalayas have no purpose of any kind – they are just there; but mechanical artefacts and organisms are different. What makes them different is that they either have been or give every appearance of having been designed. To understand such objects fully, it is not difficult to see that we need to know what they are for; and knowing what something is for is knowing about its function(s).

Returning to our example of a car, functional analysis leads us to a consideration of people's transportation needs. It is because cars display (more-or-less) good design as vehicles that they require functional explanation. Organisms display good design too. Just like cars, people possess a size, shape, power unit(s), and internal layout that go together to enable them to move around easily and efficiently (far more efficiently, incidentally, than any known car). The purpose for which cars move about is, as we have seen, quite clear; but what is the purpose of human movement? The answer is that, along with all the rest of our biological design features, the purpose of this capability is the promotion of our own or our close relatives' reproductive success. If cars and all other artefacts are for us, we and all other organisms are for reproduction; and we are this way, not because somebody else has designed us, but because we have evolved by natural selection.

Any aspect of an organism may be analysed functionally, just as any aspect may be analysed causally. Having said this, however, it is important to note that although everything about an organism must necessarily have a cause, not everything about it must necessarily have a function; strictly speaking, only those (caused) characteristics that have been or are the targets of natural selection have functions. The question 'how many of an organism's observed characteristics are functional?' is contentious, particularly in view of the finding of molecular biologists that a great deal of DNA is apparently without function, and that a great deal of the genetic variation between organisms may be the result of random processes. Although this issue is important, we shall not discuss it further here.

We are entitled to ask not only how behaviour works but also what it is for. As we have seen, this will involve us in determining how and to what extent behaviour promotes an actor's own or its close relatives' reproductive success. Behavioural ecology, evolutionary ethology, and sociobiology (the terms are more or less interchangeable) are centrally concerned with questions of this kind. The sort of insight we gain from these disciplines is rather like that which we experience when we discover the relationship between a person's actions and their intentions ('Oh, now I see why he did that!'). We must be careful to remember, though, that conscious intentions play no part in the functional analysis of behaviour. The point is not to discover what an animal aims or intends to do, but to see how what it does has enabled its lineage to persist through many generations of successful reproduction.

What isn't the question?

Applied to human behaviour, this functional approach may appear somewhat bleak. Are all of our evolved behavioural capacities really to be explained in terms of the promotion of individuals' own or their close relatives' reproductive success? The answer, very probably, is yes; but as the first half of this chapter has attempted to explain, such an answer should not be understood to carry with it any of the depressing or distressing conclusions with which it is commonly associated. To repeat: evolved behaviour is not by this token any more fundamental, any more fatal, or any more flawed than behaviour that is quite unrelated to the immediate circumstances of our biological origins.

If we were to conclude, for example, that a certain kind of aggressive behaviour had been functional in humans in their evolutionary past, and that it represented an evolved human behavioural adaptation, this would not tell us: (1) whether such aggression is to be found in all, some, or even any contemporary human societies; (2) whether, given that it occurs, it is functional in any particular cultural environment other than the one in which it evolved; (3) whether, given that it occurs, learning is or is not involved in its development; or (4) whether, how, when, or why it could or should be changed. All that it would tell us is that a tendency to respond with a certain kind of aggressive behaviour under certain specified circumstances had been naturally selected for among our evolutionary ancestors – full stop! It is the inability or unwillingness to put a full stop where it belongs in this sentence that leads so many people to see an evolutionary perspective on human behaviour as being morally or politically bleak.

History

What is the question?

There is a close connection between the study of function and the study of history. Consider once again our example of a car. Knowing what cars are for, we can work out the various functions of the different components and systems of which they are constructed; but if we want to know why these particular components and systems have been chosen to do the job, we shall find ourselves needing to know something about the history of automobile design and manufacture over the past century. The point here, of course, is that different designers, starting with different technologies, might produce vehicles radically different from those that we see today. A complete understanding of a car requires, therefore, an understanding of its pedigree.

Exactly the same principle applies to living organisms. Take, for example, fish-like animals. There are strict functional requirements to be met by any animal that makes a living by swimming around in water after its food. These requirements have been met by several different lineages that have 'converged' upon a generally fish-like body form from quite separate evolutionary starting points. If we want to know why an ichthyosaur, a shark, and a dolphin have the kinds of similarities and differences they do, then we must take into account not only the similar functional adaptations that they possess but also the dissimilar evolutionary histories by which they have come to possess them.

Again, this sort of analysis may be applied as much to behaviour as to body form. The study of behavioural similarities and differences in a group of related species may enable the comparative ethologist to trace evolutionary relationships in essentially the same way as would a comparative anatomist. Thus, on the basis of his analysis of display movements in the duck subfamily Anatinae, Konrad Lorenz (1941) revised the evolutionary classification of the group as a whole. Often, behaviour is a more reliable guide to relationships than anatomy. For example, although there is no anatomical feature that distinguishes the pigeon family Columbidae, the group may be defined by reference to a behavioural character - namely, the use of sucking movements during drinking.

Aggression can often be analysed in this way. In his comparative study of the behaviour of gulls, for example, Niko Tinbergen (1959) identified and traced the evolutionary relationships among no less than five separable displays involved in conflict behaviour; not all gulls possessed all displays, and the distribution of displays in the group reflected both functional and historical constraints. Similarly, J. van Hooff (1967) analysed the facial expressions of monkeys and apes, suggesting that some fairly well-defined 'display faces' were related to a variety of equally well-defined social behaviour patterns, such as 'approach', 'attack', and 'flee'. Van Hooff, like Tinbergen before him, aimed to trace the evolution of such display faces through the primate series; and this he did in a later paper on the phylogeny of human laughter and smiling (van Hooff 1972).

What isn't the question?

The same sort of confusion surrounds the study of history as surrounds the study of function. First, we should be clear that these two types of study are distinct, albeit closely related. During evolution, the same organ or behaviour may come to serve different functions, and different organs or behaviour may come to serve the same function. Knowing that behaviour X has an evolutionary history does not tell us what, if any, function it serves today; it does not tell us whether it is rare or common in the species, easy or hard to change, dependent or independent of any particular environmental influence. The human ethologist Irenaus Eibl-

Eibesfeldt (1979) suggests that, because aggression is an evolved 'innate' human behavioural predisposition, society must find ways of diverting its inevitable expression into constructive rather than destructive channels. This essentially Lorenzian argument so thoroughly confuses evolution and development that we despair of the possibility of extracting anything useful from it at all.

Development

What is the question?

Where evolutionists consider the history of a lineage over many generations, developmental biologists and psychologists concern themselves with the history of an individual over its lifespan. To make use of our analogy with a car for a fourth and last time, they ask the kind of question that would interest a person visiting a car factory for the first time. How does a single, harmoniously functioning machine come into being from a mass of apparently disorganized components? What is the relationship between design, blueprints, components, and assembly line; and what about the problem of quality control? From first inspiration to final inspection, the developmentally inclined car mechanic is interested in the coming-into-being of functional machinery from its constituent, largely non-functional parts.

Arguably, our mechanical analogy is at its weakest in the study of organic development. It is customary to compare the role of genes in development with that of a blueprint, and the role of environment with that of an assembly line or factory; but this analogy is very misleading. For one thing, there are clear one-to-one correspondences between blueprints and completed artefacts; but no such correspondences exist between genes and parts (or even processes) in organic development. For just as organisms are not really designed but rather come into existence through a process of evolution by natural selection, so, too, they are not really assembled from dysfunctional parts but rather come into existence through a process of gene–environment and organism–environment interaction. Secondary textbooks and most popular writing on the subject notwithstanding, these latter processes are not really very much like anything else we know of in either the natural or the artificial worlds.

For this reason (and reversing the history of most other branches of biology), it is sometimes suggested that baking may be a rather better analogy for development than manufacture. In baking, a recipe is usually followed. This recipe provides step-by-step instructions for a series of manipulations that result in, say, a cake. There is no one-to-one correspondence between items in the recipe and parts or processes in the cake; but changes in part or all of the recipe, the ingredients, the mixing, or the cooking may lead to changes in the whole cake. If we were to accept this analogy, genes would have to be regarded as instructions for the generation of organisms within a specified set of environments; and, this would allow us to accomodate the fact that, despite the lack of one-to-one correspondence noted above, changes in either the genes or their environments may result in changes in the finished organism.

It seems right to say that a developing organism is more like a cake in the baking than it is like a car in the making; but the analogy is still far from perfect. Perhaps its most serious limitation is connected with the fact that, however often they are consulted, recipes are still extraneous to cakes themselves, whereas genes are intrinsic to organisms. Where recipes are instructions for what to do to ingredients, genes are physical objects capable of participating in development only when they are part of a functioning gene–environment system. That part of their work within the cell may be likened to the process of instruction must not be allowed to blind us to the fact that, unlike recipes, genes can be regulated by the very cake whose baking they are supposed to be instructing. So much, we may say, for analogies!

What isn't the question?

It was pointed out by Pittendrigh (1958) that evolution is 'opportunistic' with respect to developmental mechanisms; that is, evolution 'makes do' with available parts and processes, 'tinkering' with them (Jacob 1983) in order to obtain new functions out of old structures. Having entered a caveat about the need not to misunderstand such anthropomorphic descriptions of the impersonal and unintelligent process of organic evolution, we can see that there is a useful insight here. For a feature to play a part in the history of a lineage, it is required only that it be present as a heritable variation in a given environment; and this, in turn, requires only that the genetic–environmental means for its development are 'tinkerable' at a given moment in evolutionary time. Most importantly, it is not required that the tinkering should result in rigidly 'hard-wired' mechanisms of the sort used in the construction of cars or computers. In fact, it is not required that the tinkering should take any particular genetic–environmental form at all, but only that it should take some available form or other.

There are many traps for the unwary student of behaviour development. One of the best-disguised is the assumption that, because a given category of behaviour such as aggression is 'natural', there will necessarily be unity and continuity in the development of such behaviour. This simply does not follow. The question of continuity in the development of early characteristics is today being closely re-examined (Brim and Kagan 1980; Hinde and Bateson 1984). Different measures of aggression, and the same measure of aggression used at different stages in development, often show relatively poor correlation with one another. We may well have to face up to the conclusion that there is no such thing as 'the (unitary) development of aggression' at all.

Goodbye to all that

In 1930, the English astronomer and physicist Sir Arthur Eddington introduced a book on *The Nature of the Physical World* by comparing the 'two tables' at which he sat as he wrote. The first table was a perfectly ordinary object, a 'common-sense' table, if you will; but the second was a quite extraordinary object, a 'scientific table', in fact. Where the former was a substantial object possessed of weight, hardness, colour, and so forth, the latter was quite insubstantial, being almost entirely composed of empty space occupied by tiny particles held together by a variety of esoteric forces. Inviting his readers to embark on a voyage of scientific discovery, therefore, Eddington told them to 'bid goodbye' to common-sense beliefs and observations about nature, 'for we are about to turn from the familiar world to the scientific world revealed by physics' (Eddington 1930).

Eddington's two tables were part of an altogether larger philosophical enterprise that does not concern us here; but his contrast between common sense and scientific beliefs about the world is extremely useful here. Ever since Copernicus advanced the idea of a sun-centred universe, physics has made progress by overthrowing seemingly obvious facts about the world; and ever since Harvey proposed his theory of the double circulation of the blood, biology has proceeded in a similar fashion. For generations, lay people and scientists alike have asked a number of common-sense questions about human aggression: Is it natural? Is it biological? Is it instinctive? Is it inevitable? Is it good for us, or bad for us? All too often, they have been tempted to answer these questions on the unspoken assumption that they make perfectly good sense scientifically speaking. This is regrettable. Vague, incoherent, and value-laden questions invite vague, incoherent, and value-laden replies; and when these replies are delivered in the language of science, they demean both the scientific and the political integrity of all parties to the dialogue.

Biological perspectives on human affairs are valid and useful. Far from offering a restrictive view of the human condition, they are a source of potentially rich and varied insights; but everything depends upon our knowing the proper scope and limits of any particular inquiry. If we ask what mechanisms subserve a particular kind of aggressive behaviour, or what functions it serves, we are not removing that behaviour from the realm of the social; conversely, if we ask how a particular kind of aggressive behaviour is learnt, or how it is or ought to be treated by parents and teachers, or lawyers and politicians, we are not removing that behaviour from the realm of the biological. Priority disputes between the biological and the social sciences are not so much unproductive as misconceived, because both disciplines have something useful to contribute at their appropriate levels of analysis.

Tinbergen's 'four whys' offer a convenient way of unpacking ideas that are contained only implicitly in common-sense questions about behaviour. There is much to be gained from a perspective in which development is seen as the integrating element among these 'four whys'. It is development, after all, that brings into existence the mechanisms that have been cumulatively selected on the grounds of their functional utility throughout the evolutionary history of a lineage. If the living world were to be seen as so many lineages of evolving developmental systems, rather than as so many 'genetically programmed survival machines', there would no longer be any need to give priority either to the genes or to the environment in our accounts of particular organic structures and functions (Oyama 1982, 1985).

Imbued with such a view, we might more easily avoid that parcelling out of behaviour – some pieces to nature, others to culture – which has caused such persistent and sterile controversy in the literature on the biology of animal and human aggression. Questions from the nature–culture tradition ('is it natural or cultural?', 'biological or social?', 'genetic or environmental?') are best avoided, not because they threaten any particular ideology, but because they carry far too much excess conceptual baggage for comfort and because they hinder productive inquiry by mixing issues better kept separate.

In subsequent chapters, we shall examine several different questions about aggression from this general perspective. Intentionally reversing the conventional order in which these questions are treated ('biological basis' first, and 'social superstructure' second), we shall review what can sensibly be said about aggression at several different levels of analysis: the cultural–anthropological, the psychological–developmental, the mechanistic–biological, and the evolutionary–biological. Because the confusions that give rise to so much contemporary argument about these topics are extremely deep-rooted, we shall return repeatedly to the themes of this chapter. Our far from easy task will be to attempt to explore the science and politics of animal and human conflict without falling victim to any of these confusions ourselves.

CHAPTER FOUR

Cultural counterpoint The social construction of anger and aggression

Doing anthropology

We have seen that there is a close correspondence between certain popular conceptions of human nature in our society and a number of influential scientific theories to do with the 'biological basis' of human behaviour. Looked at from an anthropological perspective, this correspondence is just what we might expect. After all, individuals are members of their own culture long before they are members of a professional community of research scientists; and it would be miraculous if they were not influenced by their culture's prevailing beliefs about nature, human nature, and society. Ironically, it is anthropologists themselves who are the most vulnerable to such influences, because it is they who study the very beliefs and practices about which all cultures (including their own) possess very deeply entrenched views. At its worst, so-called 'ethnocentrism' can lead to a situation in which expert anthropological judgements may tell us more about the society to which anthropologists belong than they do about the societies to which they explicitly refer.

This chapter is about the contribution that anthropology has made, and could yet make, to our understanding of anger and aggression. Hitherto, our own culture's folk model of aggressive behaviour has played too great a part in anthropological interpretations of other cultures. Yet there are clues in the existing anthropological literature to other and quite different folk models, developed in the context of other and quite different cultural experiences. These provide a possible basis for an approach that transcends the rather barren stereotypes of so much that is still written about human aggression from an overwhelmingly Western cultural perspective.

It is conventional to distinguish between 'physical anthropology' (broadly speaking, the study of human biology, and particularly of human evolution) and 'social anthropology' (broadly speaking, the study of the diversity of human cultural beliefs and practices; in the United States, this latter discipline is usually called 'cultural anthropology'). The very existence of this distinction testifies to the polarization that exists in our thinking between 'nature' and 'culture'; and, of course, for many purposes it is both artificial and unhelpful. Nevertheless, simply because most anthropologists come to the problem of human conflict from one or other of these two very different orientations, we shall abide by the distinction here. We shall begin by saying something about physical-anthropological perspectives on human aggression, and then go on to consider at rather greater length the surprisingly similar issues that are raised by cultural–anthropological approaches to the same problem.

Interpreting the bones

In the century or so since Charles Darwin surveyed *The Descent of Man* (1871), physical anthropology has made great strides in assembling evidence relevant to an understanding of human origins. Thanks to the dedicated efforts of a relatively small number of hunters after the so-called 'missing link' (Reader 1981), we possess today a far better fossil record of our animal ancestry than anyone in Darwin's day had the right even to hope for, let alone to expect. Moreover, in combination with equally spectacular developments in fields such as molecular biology and primatology, this fossil record is now being made to yield reasonably firm conclusions regarding the evolutionary relationships among the great apes and humans. Today, for example, it is very widely agreed that our closest living relatives are the chimpanzees and the gorilla, and that the last common ancestor of these apes and ourselves lived in Africa somewhere between 4.5 and 7.5 million years ago (for a clear and entertaining guide to the relevant evidence, see Zihlman 1982).

This having been said, however, it must also be acknowledged that in the century or so since Darwin, sparse and often ambiguous data have frequently been poured with comparative ease into the moulds of prevailing prejudices about humankind. In particular, evidence relating to human origins has been made repeatedly to deliver all-too-familiar conclusions about human nature and human aggression. Typical of the sorts of interpretation that have been on offer are the views of the prominent early twentieth-century British palaeoanthropologist, Sir Arthur Keith. In the wake of the Second World War, Keith proposed that the key to human origins lay in a process of natural selection amongst our earliest ancestors for genocidal intergroup aggression. This it was, he argued, that underlay the otherwise mysterious expansion of the brain and intelligence, culminating in the emergence of an extremely bright but also extremely combative and war-like *Homo sapiens* (Keith 1949).

This theme was soon taken up by the anatomist Raymond Dart (1954), who claimed to find on many damaged fossil hominid bones from southern African sites clear evidence of prehistoric homicide. It was from Dart that the playwright Robert Ardrey took the idea of our ancestors as 'killer apes', and turned it into the best-selling theme of a succession of popular books. The opening declaration of Ardrey's first book on this subject, *African Genesis*, virtually said it all: 'Not in Asia', it asserted, 'and not in innocence, was mankind born.' According to Ardrey, the romantic idea of human perfectibility had been decisively refuted by recent developments in palaeoanthropology and primatology, developments which demonstrated that, as he put it, 'We are Cain's children, all of us' (Ardrey 1961). Of course, what Ardrey was doing with powerful rhetoric such as this was offering up in a new form an old religious myth regarding the human condition. With striking consistency, he presented his scientific thesis concerning the evolved aggressiveness of human nature in the images and metaphors of the Christian doctrine of 'original sin'. As other authors took up his message throughout the 1960s, what was little more than a common cultural prejudice was made to appear as if it were the authentic voice of science; and, for several years, it really appeared as if the fossil record would be forced irrevocably into the mould of 'original sin'.

Fortunately, this did not happen. From the very beginning, there were anthropologists and biologists who recognized very clearly what was going on (see, for example, Montagu 1968); and over the past decade there have been several important attempts to set the record straight. Thus, for example, Richard Leakey is but one among a growing number of fossil hunters who have argued in recent years that the idea of humans as 'killer apes' is completely unfounded. Indeed, he has suggested that it is 'one of the most dangerously persuasive myths of our time' (Leakey and Lewin 1977). Extending the same theme, several women palaeoanthropologists have suggested that their profession's apparent obsession with early hominid aggression and warfare is the product of a systematic and distorting male bias in the literature. As Leakey has argued that the fossil record is more compatible with a peaceable than it is with a violent scenario of early hominid evolution (Leakey and Lewin 1977, 1979; Leakey 1981), so Nancy Tanner and Adrienne Zihlman have constructed a model in which cooperative relationships among women and children, rather than competitive relationships among men, were central to the emergence of our species (Tanner and Zihlman 1976; Tanner 1981).

Today, it is generally recognized that the 'killer ape' hypothesis is a totally inadequate interpretation of the evidence. To take just one example, it has been shown that the damaged bones that Dart and others took for the results of early hominid aggression are far better explained by processes such as leopard predation (Brain 1981); but even such admittedly important reinterpretations as this do not get quite to the heart of the problem. For suppose, just for the sake of argument, that the evidence had gone the other way. Would this have allowed us to draw any firm conclusions about the aggressive natures of our hominid ancestors? Of course not.

To see why this is so, consider another case in which very similar evidence does appear to go the other way. It has been known for several decades that some of the skulls of *Homo erectus* from Zhoukoudian (Choukoutien), China give every indication of having been intentionally damaged around the foramen magnum (the hole at the base of the skull through which the spinal cord enters the cranium). In this case, it has been suggested that the damage may have been connected with the extraction and eating of the brain; but before jumping to the conclusion that our ancestors were 'innately aggressive' towards one another, we would do well to recall that several living hunter–gatherer communities are known to practise so-called 'endo-cannibalism' (i.e., the eating of members of their own social group). Very often, however, this is done as a way of venerating or acquiring the virtue of deceased relatives and friends; and this, whatever else we may think of it, can hardly be counted as a form of interpersonal aggression.

The important point here is that an adequate interpretation of human behaviour depends crucially upon a knowledge of the cultural context within which it is occurring. Without such knowledge, it is often impossible to tell what may be the true nature of even the most apparently brutal of behavioural activities. Is the eating of another person's body aggressive or appeasing? Is it the expression of hunger, of anger, or of grief? From the bones alone, and even granting that we can deduce from them reasonably firm conclusions about some aspect of early hominid behaviour, it is often impossible to distinguish between alternatives such as these; in other words, it is often impossible to bridge the gulf between behaviour (i.e., what people do) and action (i.e., the personal and interpersonal meaning of what they do) (Harré and Secord 1973; Reynolds 1976). For this reason alone, all palaeoanthropological claims regarding prehistoric human nature must be treated with the greatest caution.

There are signs in the recent literature of a move towards a genuinely contextual approach to human behaviour among some palaeoanthropologists (for a review, see Isaac 1983). However, these are just the beginnings of what promises to be a useful approach; and it would be premature to try to found any very significant conclusions upon them yet.

Instead, the obvious place to look for insight into the cultural context of human behaviour is social rather than physical anthropology. After all, it is the job of social anthropologists to 'get beneath the skin' of the people they study in an effort to unravel the symbolic significance of what they do. Even here, as we shall see, the attribution of meaning may be far from easy; but at least there is a substantial body of relevant evidence upon which to draw.

In the remainder of this chapter, we shall consider both the problems that are involved in the interpretation of cultures and the insights that such interpretation provides into the construction of individual anger and aggression within society.

Street scene

> *Nov. 23, 1973.* Hartford, Connecticut. Three policemen giving a heart massage and oxygen to a heart attack victim on Friday were attacked by a crowd of 75 to 100 persons who apparently did not realize what the policemen were doing.
>
> Other policemen fended off the crowd of mostly Spanish-speaking residents until an ambulance arrived. Police said they tried to explain to the crowd what they were doing, but the crowd apparently thought they were beating the woman.
>
> Despite the policemen's efforts the victim, Evangelica Echevacria, 59, died (*The Minneapolis Tribune*; quoted in Spradley 1980, pp. 6–7).

Here we have a single, dramatic event that can be interpreted in many ways. Almost certainly, a basic knowledge of modern medical techniques, together with a basic trust in the processes of law enforcement, would have made most North American bystanders rather well-disposed towards the three policemen struggling to save the heart-attack victim on the street; but to the Hispanics who actually witnessed the scene, these men appeared not as heroes but as villains. Obviously, the Hispanics viewed what was happening through the lens of a culture and a history very different from those of most North Americans. Perhaps they were heirs to a medical tradition in which treatment of heart-attack victims takes a different, less-violent form; or perhaps they had recently suffered from police brutality against their community in that neighbourhood. Whatever the truth of the matter, however, this example demonstrates that a single event may have more than one 'common-sense' interpretation.

It is often said that 'seeing is believing'; but seeing is as much a cultural as it is a physiological and a psychological process. Seeing really is a matter of *common* sense – that is, of shared perceptions. Of course, individuals may change their view of things in the light of experience; and groups, too, may adjust to new situations by modifying or even totally reorganizing their 'common-sense' beliefs about the world. Thus, it is conceivable that some of those who witnessed the attempted resuscitation at Hartford, Connecticut actually learned something that challenged their earlier opinions about medicine or the police; and it is also possible that the policemen themselves learned something that challenged their earlier opinions about the Hispanic community. On another occasion, perhaps one of the spectators might stop a friend from 'rescuing' a heart-attack victim from her helpers; and perhaps the policemen involved might be able to depend on a better relationship with the Hispanic community as they explain what they are trying to do. Individuals can and do modify their ideas about the world through time; and as individuals change, so do the cultures to which they belong. Nevertheless, the power of collective representations over individual experience of the world can be very great.

We need to challenge our own common-sense views of human conflict. These views are a distinctive product of modern Western culture, and precisely because they are so deeply entrenched in our way of thinking about the world we find it difficult always to maintain the important distinction between these views and the world to which they are meant to refer. But different cultures think about conflict very differently; and for this reason, a cross-cultural perspective can help not merely to cut our own ideas down to size but also to show how we humans construct our knowledge out of the interactive relationship between thought and experience in society. If in what follows we appear to spend an inordinate amount of time reviewing relatively familiar, Western concepts relating to aggression, this is because it is vitally important to subject to scrutiny those things that we are most inclined simply to take for granted.

Anger and aggression in Western culture

You are late leaving the house for work, the traffic is very thick today, the coffee you pick up when you arrive at the office is cold, and the work you left for your secretary to get on with in your absence needs completely redoing. At each added insult you feel the pressure rising. Perhaps you merely grit your teeth; but as the day wears on, and difficulties continue to occur, you develop a headache, or possibly your ulcer begins to play up.

Finally, the day is done and you return home, only to find that your husband has forgotten to prepare an evening meal. You mutter, 'I can't stand it any more, I've had enough!' Depending on your character and your relationships with your family, you may do one or other of the following things: cry; yell; kick the dog; take it out on the children; dig the garden; or go out and drown your sorrows with a friend. Why not? Surely these are all 'natural' reactions to what has been, after all, an unreasonably bad day?

We operate with several different and only partially consistent folk models of aggression. One such model is based upon the notion that aggression is caused by anger, an emotion that is commonly regarded as existing within us, rather like some sort of alien being that is capable of acting independently of our reason or our will. This notion is part of a more general Western view that sees emotions as physical forces; these, when strong enough, may impel or even compel conduct for which the actor can scarcely be regarded as responsible. We are all familiar with the idea of people being 'carried away by their emotions'; and the idea of a 'crime of passion' has a secure place not only in popular parlance but even in some Western legal systems. Similarly, when it comes to aggression, who has not heard someone say, 'I couldn't help myself, I was so angry . . .'?

Linked to this view of anger as a force or a being within us is the idea that it may accumulate over time, or under provocation, to the point where perhaps the final response is both inevitable and out of all proportion with the immediate cause. We speak of our feelings 'welling up inside' us, and of our 'pent-up emotions'; and we imagine some sort of accumulating reservoir of anger seeking release. Moreover, we believe that the fullness of this reservoir has physiological consequences. As in our example above, it may be associated not only with the familiar red face and tense muscles of belligerence but also, perhaps, with the headache or the ulcer of frustrated fury.

The 'anger causes aggression' model, which is so much a part of our common-sense Western cultural view, rests on important assumptions about the relationship between physiological and psychological causes of emotion. These assumptions emerge, for example, in the way in which we use the word 'feeling' to describe a great variety of experiences. We 'feel' objects or pinpricks; we 'feel' hunger or fatigue; we 'feel' love or anger; and we even 'feel' loyal or patriotic. Clearly, quite a lot of very different things are being lumped together here; and there is a temptation to assign similar causes to them all. Thus, simply because the 'feeling' of objects or pinpricks appears to have specific physiological causes in the peripheral nervous system that are quite unrelated to any conscious thought or decision on our part, it may appear as if the 'feeling' of love or anger, loyalty, or patriotism must have similar physiological causes as well. This, in part, is how we have constructed the idea of anger as an internal cause of aggression that is more or less beyond our conscious control.

While we are dealing with common-sense Western ideas about anger and aggression, it is worth pointing out that these are linked to other Western notions about the nature and causes of warfare. Pretty obviously, wars are not literally caused by personal anger. Those who plan and orchestrate them may be as much or more moved by cool-headed economic and political calculations as they are by hot-headed feelings of righteous indignation; and those who actually have to go out and fight in them may be more afraid than they are angry. Indeed, it has been claimed that, during the First World War, men in the frontline trenches had often to be cajoled or duped into continuing to shoot at one another over extended periods of time (Axelrod 1984).

Nonetheless, there is a connection between anger, aggression, and warfare; this connection, however, is largely metaphorical. It may be seen, for example, in the way in which we use the language of 'conflict' or 'fighting' to cover both small-scale, personal and large-scale, group interactions; and it is especially obvious in the way in which we use the same strategic language to describe everything from the playing of games and the winning of debates to the conduct of military campaigns (Lakoff and Johnson 1981). Moreover, the metaphors of anger and personal conflict are often used to mobilize populations for war. During a war effort, governments may try to incite general animosity among the populace against 'the enemy' (notice the use of the singular noun); and officers may exhort their troops to hate all 'Jerries', or whomever, by caricaturing them as evil, ugly brutes. In extending to collective military endeavour well-established ideas about individual anger and aggression, we foster the notion that war is also an inevitable outcome of uncontrollable forces from within.

Anger and aggression in Western anthropology

How far has our Western folk model of anger and aggression found its way into the efforts of Western anthropologists to interpret patterns of conflict in their own and other cultures? We do not have space to answer this question in any great detail, but with the help of just a single example we shall try to show that the popular conception of anger as an internal and an inevitable cause of aggression does find expression in the writings of some Western anthropologists. On occasions, as we shall see, this conception can generate some quite extraordinary interpretations of cultures, which are very different from our own.

The theme of a 'biological foundation' for aggression is well illustrated in the biological anthropologist Melvin Konner's recent big book, *The Tangled Wing: Biological Constraints on the Human Spirit* (1982). This book devotes a chapter to 'Rage'. Explicitly enlisting Freud in support of his version of the 'anger (= rage) causes aggression' model discussed above, Konner sets out the case for the existence of 'innate aggressive tendencies in humans' (Konner 1982). In doing so, he refers to Robert K. Dentan's work on the Semai people in Malaysia. Superficially, these people appear to constitute a counter-instance to Konner's thesis. Dentan reports that the Semai are normally non-violent. They rarely strike each other, and war had seemed to them a rather improbable fancy before they came into contact with the British. According to Dentan, they had never participated in armed conflict until the British recruited some of their young men to help fight against the Communist rebels in the 1950s. Once these young men had been organized and trained, however, Dentan reports that they became not merely good soldiers but positively bloodthirsty combatants. As given (inaccurately) by Konner, Dentan quotes a veteran of one campaign as follows: 'We killed, killed, killed. The Malays would stop and go through people's pockets and take their watches and money. We did not think of watches or money. We only thought of killing. Wah, truly we were drunk with blood' (Konner 1982, p.207).

On the basis of this and similar quotations, Konner concludes his chapter on rage with the theme that, while cultural conditioning may modify or suppress a basic human capacity of violence, it can never eliminate it altogether: 'What seems certain to me', he writes, ' . . . is that no cultural training, however designed, can eliminate the basic core of capability of violence that is part of the makeup of human beings' (Konner 1982, p.207).

What are we to make of this conclusion? Superficially, it seems almost platitudinous. After all, who could possibly wish to deny the obvious fact that all normal humans possess a 'capability of violence'? At this level, one might mount arguments analogous to Konner's about many other interesting features of Semai behaviour. Thus, we might point out that the Semai had never marched up and down in close ranks before, owing entirely to their cultural training; but that the influence of the British proved conclusively that they possessed a biological capability for marching up and down in close ranks, a capability that no amount of cultural training could entirely abolish. The point is, of course, that there is a theoretically infinite list of things that the Semai (and all humans) have a common capacity to do; and there really does not seem to be a great deal to be gained simply by listing them.

Clearly, this is not quite all that Konner means to say here. For it is in the notion that the Semai possess not merely a capability of violence but rather a 'basic core of capability of violence' that his argument gains whatever non-truistic force it may be said to possess. Once again, we are back with the idea that particular kinds of overt behaviour are in some sense more basic (because more fundamentally biological) than others. But what is it about the Semai, or for that matter anyone else, that justifies a conclusion regarding the distinction between 'basic' and 'superficial' behavioural attributes in humans? By using exactly the same data as Konner, but interpreting it differently, it is easy to show that this added claim about a 'core' of capability of violence is entirely redundant.

Consider again the two facts that may be obtained from Dentan's work: first, the Semai are usually non-violent and think of human nature as non-violent; and secondly, under the military control of a colonial power, they were trained for a war into which they plunged by indulging in a frenzy of killing. Now it is quite clear from Dentan's report that the Semai viewed the fighting in which they had become caught up as a kind of drunkenness or madness; apparently, they were 'bemused' by their own behaviour (Dentan 1979). Why should we not conclude, therefore, that the Semai are 'basically' non-violent? After all, it was only when they were removed from their normal environment and subjected to a definite process of cultural training that they could be persuaded to indulge in warfare; and even then, they did not seem either to learn the rules properly or to understand what was happening to them.

Of course, we have no more justification for our new interpretation than Konner had for his. The point of this exercise is not to invert Konner's original thesis but rather to indicate that to ask which state of the Semai, the non-violent or the violent, is the more basic is a trick question. Neither the capacity for non-violence nor the capacity for violence has any kind of ontological priority, the one over the other; and we are gaining only the illusion of greater understanding by indulging in verbal games of this kind. To command a hearing, a science of human behaviour must surely be capable of a great deal more than this.

Works such as Konner's are bound by the Western cultural assumption that a distinct biological base is the key constituent of human nature, with all the rest being merely tacked on by personal whim, cultural pressure, or whatever. There are no cogent scientific reasons for viewing things this way. Of course, there are useful scientific distinctions to be made among human behavioural attributes – such as, for example, the distinction between those behavioural attributes that represent evolved adaptations and those that do not; but the ever-popular distinction between human nature and human culture, with the former seen as a biological base and the latter as a learnt superstructure, has no plausible technical meaning or theoretical use. It persists in the literature, not for scientific reasons, but rather because it is a fundamental element in our own culture's way of making sense of the world. For this reason, if for no other, it seems important to recognize that there is a plurality of such ways of making sense of the world. It is to the job of doing justice to them, free (so far as possible) from the constraints of our own preconceptions, that we turn next.

A different emotional quality from our own

Understanding what is going on in a culture very different from our own can be extremely difficult. It is hard enough simply to learn a foreign language, but getting to grips with how people from other cultures actually feel and think about their own experience may be next to impossible for us to achieve. However, we should not let this discourage us. Even though we may not be able to achieve a perfect understanding of the lives of other peoples, we may at least be able to get far enough along the path of empathetic observation to recognize the inadequacy of our own concepts to the explanation of their behaviour.

Imagine yourself at the 'Gisaro ceremony' among the Kaluli people of Papua New Guinea. It is the middle of the night, and you are one of many spectators sitting on a sleeping platform in a longhouse. The scene is only dimly lit by the six torches held by young men near the front. Without warning, four dancers appear, their bodies decorated spectacularly with red and black paint, large tropical bird feathers, jewellery, and huge tails made of stripped palm leaves. One dancer performs at a time. Lightly bouncing up and down with a rattle, the first begins to sing a quiet song in a minor key. If you have learned the language, you will notice that the song refers to recently deceased family and friends of the host clan, together with the places where these people lived and worked. Suddenly, a man in the audience, wailing and tearful, leaps up, snatches a torch, and hits the dancer's shoulders with its burning end. Now, all the young men of the host community jump about and make a great deal of noise. The singer continues his song, accompanied by a chorus of his fellow dancers; and then the entire scene is repeated over and over, with each dancer taking turns at performing. The Gisaro ceremony does not end until daybreak, when the dancers pay compensation to all whom they made cry during the night. As you walk out into the tropical dawn, the woman who was sitting next to you comments, 'Many people wept. That was a very good Gisaro ceremony'.

Surely the Gisaro ceremony resembles no organized entertainment available in our culture – unless, that is, we count as entertainment certain of the more bizarre forms of group therapy available in some parts of the United States. The themes represented in the Gisaro ceremony are as obvious to the Kaluli as that of the 'eternal triangle' in television soap operas is to Westerners; but to us they appear strange and even mysterious. Of course, we may decide that the best way of getting beneath this appearance is to apply to the Gisaro ceremony our own notions of aggression. Perhaps the ceremony is really some sort of catharsis, a release of stored up 'tensions', a Kaluli analogue of our football games? This would certainly account for the Kaluli's feeling that, however violent, the ceremony is good for the community; and it would also help to explain the fact that attacks on the dancers are said to be compliments to their skills.

There is a familiar difficulty to do with the explanatory status of concepts such as catharsis. Beyond this, however, there is another and more profound problem with this explanation. For almost certainly, the Kaluli emotions that we label as 'sadness', 'anger', and so forth do not correspond with our own sadness and anger; instead, they appear to have a different subjective quality and a different social meaning. This implies that we may radically mistake the nature of the Gisaro ceremony if we content ourselves merely with analogies to more familiar practices in our own culture, together with the appropriate Western explanatory devices. Instead, to learn more about the Gisaro we must learn more about Kaluli emotion; and to do that, we must study the ceremony in relation to everyday life in Kaluli culture as a whole (Schieffelin 1976; Feld 1982). If we were to undertake such a study, we should soon discover that the Kaluli's experience of and knowledge about the world are very different from ours; and that, as a result, their conception of human nature is quite foreign to us. Not only do different things make Kaluli people sad or angry, but the emotional experiences associated with sadness and anger appear to be different from what we might have expected.

Schieffelin (1973, pp. 183–4), for example, reports as follows:

> When Kaluli feel strongly about something, they are not usually ones to hide their feelings. Rage, grief, dismay, embarrassment, fear, and compassion may be openly and often dramatically expressed. Frequently, the intent seems aimed at influencing others, whether by intimidating them (e.g., with anger) or by evoking their compassion and support (e.g., with grief). A man whose expectations have been frustrated or who has suffered a

wrong or injury at the hands of others does not usually suppress his annoyance. Rather he is likely to orchestrate his anger into a splendid frightening rage, projecting himself with threats and recriminations against his (often equally angry) opponent in a volatile exercise of social brinkmanship that occasionally leads to violence. Similarly, dismay or grief might be openly expressed, often evoking others' sympathy and support. These displays of affect have to be seen more as declarations of mind, motivation, and/or intention than as mere cathartic expressions of feeling.

This view of Kaluli emotion is radically different from that used by biological anthropologists such as Konner. Schieffelin's reference to the 'orchestration of anger' and his insistence that Kaluli displays of affect must be seen as 'declarations of mind' together reveal a view of emotions as intentional constructs rather than physical universals. In other words, for Schieffelin emotions are not things that happen to people; they are not alien powers of forces that from time to time intrude upon the otherwise smooth flow of purposeful human actions. On the contrary, emotions are actively mobilized resources that are deployed by individuals in their attempts to achieve particular objects in social life.

It is surely significant that, with rare and honourable exceptions, emotional experience has been generally ignored in cultural studies; for in accordance with the Western folk model, it has been treated as a biological constant across cultures. Here, however, Schieffelin provides a useful lead into an exploration of the way in which emotions may develop within specific cultural contexts, just as knowledge and beliefs are known to do.

'Anger' and 'aggression' among the Utku Eskimo

In her ethnography of the Utkuhikhalingmiut, or Utku Eskimos, the anthropologist Jean Briggs (1970) has given us a rare glimpse of emotional life within another culture. Her work provides a great deal of linguistic data, together with rich descriptions of personal interactions among the people; and from this information, it is possible to go some way towards reconstructing the forms of Utku 'anger' and 'aggression'. Significantly, these turn out to be rather different from our own.

The Utku are a small nomadic band of 20–35 people who, in the course of their travels, occupy a total area of 35,000 square miles in the Canadian North West Territories, north of Hudson Bay. Moving, which appears to be a happy and an exciting event, occurs with the seasons, according to the availability of food animals (the Utku hunt fox, seal, and caribou). Iglus are built in winter, and then as ice turns to slush the band moves and establishes summer tents. There are no formal leaders, and social structure appears to revolve primarily around close interactions between a relatively small number of family households.

The Utku are a generally peaceable and non-violent people. They condemn what we could call angry feelings and aggressive behaviour, and they appear to value love and nurturance above all else. Indeed, angry thoughts alone, even where these may never be expressed, are considered dangerous and even potentially lethal. Despite the smoothness of their everyday lives, however, the Utku do not deny 'aggression'. But they conceive of it in a manner quite different from that to which most of us are accustomed. For not only does the Utku conception of aggression involve the notion of intent, but also it incorporates the ideas of withdrawal from the group and refusal to share.

According to Briggs's data, the Utku have no noun equivalent to our word 'anger', but only verbs describing angry feeling/thinking and aggressive behaviour. They also have a word, *qiquq*, which Briggs translates as 'being clogged up'. This appears to suggest our notion of 'pent-up anger'. Briggs (1970, p. 333) writes as follows:

> *Qiquq* in its physical sense is applied to objects such as iglu ventilators, fishing holes, and primus nipples, which get, quite literally, clogged up and have to be cleaned out. In its emotional sense, the behavior most often labelled *qiquq* in my experience was sulky, silent withdrawal. ... Signs of imminent tears were also labelled *qiquq*.

Briggs suggests that *qiquq* is associated with childishness, and is typically a response to not receiving enough of some coveted good (be it attention, food, or whatever). It is important to note that *qiquq* is quite different from our notions of frustration or anger; as Briggs describes it, the word is used with reference to a form of behaviour, rather than an internal feeling state. The latter is expressed better by *ningaq*, which may be translated as to think angrily or to aggress physically; but even that term is used primarily with reference to behaviour. Neither *qiquq* nor *ningaq* carry any implications regarding the possibility of explosive violence, as our word anger so often does; indeed, *qiquq* behaviour is mostly passive, including even depressive withdrawal. Moreover, the 'cure' for *qiquq*, especially in children, is not catharsis but rather the development of greater reason and maturity (*ilhuma*). Adults who are *qiquq*, *ningaq*, or otherwise inappropriately or threateningly out of sorts, are simply teased, ignored, or ostracized.

If we were to ask the Utku why children occasionally act in ways that we would describe as aggressive, they would say that children are not yet fully developed. The normal adult develops an equable temperament 'naturally' (!), and, just as any adult who tends towards inappropriate laughter or fear is considered to be childish, so any adult who expresses too much bad temper is expected simply to grow up. The Utku never find what we term aggressiveness a good quality; bad temper is always disapproved of, and even personal intensity or dominance that involves no temper at all are considered either amusing or frightening.

Jean Briggs's initial plan for fieldwork was to study shamanism amongst Eskimos, but upon arrival she found that all shamanistic practices had been firmly discarded in favour of devout Anglicanism (missionaries had made their first contact with the Utku 30 years earlier). Interestingly, the religious preaching and teaching that was occasionally directed at her revealed how a version of Western Christianity had been translated so as to conform to a generally pacific way of life. One day, for example, Briggs's adopted father said, 'God loves us and wants us to belong to him. Satan also wants us. He takes people who get angry easily (*urulu, ningaq*), and puts them in a fiery place. ... We don't get angry here' (Briggs 1970).

The point of this example drawn from another language and another way of life is that the concepts of 'anger' and 'aggression' are culturally constructed. The Utku live very differently from us, and they have knowledge and beliefs about the world that are very different from ours. Part of this different thought and practice is a set of ideas relating to emotional behaviour with which we may find it difficult to empathize. There is no way for us to know what it is 'really' like to be an Utku Eskimo – apart, that is, from abandoning our own culture and joining theirs; but the grammar and vocabulary of Utku emotion, together with the grammar and vocabulary of Utku 'common-sense' beliefs about personal relationships, are enough to indicate that our own culture's ideas about anger and aggression do not apply to them in any straightforward or simple way.

Reconstructing anger and aggression

We shall not attempt to formulate a concrete alternative to the 'anger causes aggression' model that we have criticized in previous sections. However, we must point out that, as in so many other areas of our subject, the chief problem to be faced here concerns the way in which the biological, the psychological, and the social interact to produce the characteristic feeling-states that accompany human action. An 'outburst' of anger (note the metaphor) is never just a particular concentration of this or that hormone circulating in the bloodstream; it is never just a particular belief regarding the actions or the intentions of others; and it is never just a particular set of cultural rules concerning what counts as appropriate conduct in any given situation. But it may very often be a particular combination of all three.

The trouble with the Western folk model is that it emphasizes the physical components of emotion to the virtual exclusion of all else. Yet the existence of a cognitive (and, hence, of a cultural) component in emotion has been recognized by some behavioural scientists for many years. For example, in an early and influential study, Schachter and Singer (1962) investigated the relationship between physiological 'arousal' and psychological 'feeling' in a group of college students. Told that they were to be given an injection of a new vitamin in order to determine its effects on vision, a group of subjects was actually given adrenalin instead, which was intended to put them into a state of general physiological arousal; another group of controls received merely an injection of saline (a harmless placebo). Subjects and controls were then divided into different test groups, exposed to two different social settings, and self-rated for 'happiness' and 'anger'. Schachter and Singer found a tendency for subjects to respond either euphorically or angrily, depending upon which emotion was suggested to them during the experiment. Significantly, those who received adrenalin experienced an enhanced response, irrespective of whether they were responding euphorically or angrily. On its own, in other words, physiological arousal was insufficient to specify emotion; what was needed in addition was a particular social-psychological context.

Very rarely, outside of psychological laboratories, do we experience sudden changes in blood adrenalin levels that are totally unrelated to social context. Normally, the physiological 'symptoms' of arousal are just that; they are a response to particular situations in which we are anxious or happy, fearful or angry. Thus, if we know that a scorpion is dangerous we may well experience both fear and a rapidly increased rate of heartbeat when we see one, but if we have never heard of scorpions we may be totally unaffected. Interestingly, in cases where physiological symptoms of arousal occur in what appear to be inappropriate situations, we may actively search for an explanation. For example, we may attribute the arousal to purely physical causes (as in, 'Hmmm, I must have had too much coffee'); or we may re-evaluate the situations themselves (as in, 'Hmmm, he must have made me angrier than I thought'). If we fail in such attempts at explanation, and if the symptoms persist, then we may even begin to wonder if we are not physically ill.

Exactly the same principle applies to the emotions themselves. In normal daily life, these are intimately related to the social contexts in which they occur. Indeed, should a person's emotions become too detached from their wider context, they soon give rise to concern, if not on the part of the person involved, then certainly on the part of their relatives and friends, who may fear that they are mentally disturbed (or, as a psychiatrist might put it, that they are suffering from an 'affective disorder'). It is only to the extent that emotions are seen as appropriate that they are accepted as an integral part of social life.

Our physiology, then, is intimately interwoven with both our knowledge and our expectations of the world around us; and these, in turn, are mediated by the cultures in which we live. Life in a culture in which *qiquq* is seen as a throwback to childhood, or a renunciation of society, is a long way from life in a culture in which anger is seen as the healthy expression of energetic independence; and the experience of aggression in each is presumably radically different. Aggression occurs outside of the specific contexts that grant it meaning and legitimacy only in those who are either very young (and hence not yet 'responsible for their actions') or very deranged (and hence have lost such responsibility). This is merely another way of saying that we are actors in our social worlds, not puppets, and that the variety of plays we perform is testimony to our creativity as the corporate playwrights of our own lives.

It is important in cross-cultural studies to sort out our own assumptions from the information at hand. Even Schieffelin and Briggs have a tendency to describe the behaviour of the societies in which they lived according to Western common-sense psychological concepts. Of course, humans do share many things in common, and it may be that at least some aspects of our taken-for-granted Western views about emotion and action, anger and aggression, will eventually prove useful in other contexts. But this is still very much an open question; and it is one that cannot in principle be answered unless these notions are, as it were, held in abeyance pending the outcome of future investigations into the ethnography of emotion. Such investigations must start with the discomfiting thought that there may be as many different ways of feeling as there are of thinking and talking.

CHAPTER FIVE

Genes, hormones, and learning
The development of aggression in animals

What makes a good show horse?

Consider for a moment the owner, breeder, and trainer of a stable of show horses. This woman has not, we may suppose, been educated as a scientist; but her goal is to produce horses that are ideally suited for a particular purpose – they must be attractive, athletic, tractable, and so on; and to this end she has at her disposal a number of well-tried techniques. First, there is selecting breeding. When choosing breeding stock, the stable owner looks not only at conformation, appearance, and movement but also at character, disposition, and temperament. Furthermore, she looks at blood lines; that is, she expects pedigree to be a useful predictor of both physique and personality. She may reject one mare simply because it comes from a line renowned for viciousness, and accept another simply because its close relations are known to be gentle.

The stable owner does not confine her attention to selective breeding. In addition, she pays close attention to the treatment and handling of foals. For example, she has her young male horses gelded (i.e., castrated) as a matter of course, except in rare cases where she wishes to keep a particular animal (or sell it) as a breeding stud. She does this, partly to ease the chores of management (removing, for example, the necessity of separating animals that are not to be bred together), and partly because, as she might put it, 'everyone knows' that stallions are generally far more difficult to handle in the show ring than are geldings.

Finally, the stable owner devotes great pains to the handling of her horses. She recognizes the importance of young foals becoming used to people and to human surroundings before they are more than a day or two old. She realizes that if she waits even until they are a week old, they will be much more fearful and difficult to approach. Young horses, she has learnt, must be taught discipline and restraint early; no one wants to deal with an unhandled adult animal. Despite individual differences, she knows that certain rules of training hold true for all horses: for example, either too little punishment or too much can result in dangerous, unmanageable animals that will be difficult either to show or to sell.

Governing all of the work of the stable owner is the knowledge that the ideal show horse, the perfect animal for which she is continually striving, is a precise combination of pedigree, treatment, and handling. This knowledge, however, is based upon principles of which she may be only dimly aware. These are: first, that both physical and behavioural differences between animals may be caused by genetic differences between them; secondly, that behavioural differences between animals may be caused by physiological, and particularly sex-hormonal, differences; and, thirdly, that behavioural differences between animals may be caused by differences in early learning and socialization.

As our example illustrates, these three principles apply as much to aggressive as to other forms of behaviour; and, together, they provide the framework for this chapter. In what follows, we shall examine some of the evidence relating to the influence of genes, hormones, and learning on the development of aggression in animals. Having done this, we shall consider the relevance of this evidence for the study of human behaviour.

Genes and aggression

When Charles Darwin was struggling to understand the mechanism of organic evolution, he was greatly struck by the way in which plant and animal breeders were able to produce new domesticated varieties. Indeed, he was so impressed by their work that he took the trouble to become something of an authority on that ever-popular English pastime, pigeon-fancying. The reason for Darwin's interest is easy to see. Knowing that selective breeding had enabled pigeon-fanciers to transform their birds almost at will, he reasoned that there might be a similar process in nature – a process by which not just new domestic varieties but rather new species might come into existence. In the end, of course, Darwin discovered such a process; and by borrowing the notion of selective breeding as a metaphor for it, he suggested the term 'natural selection' (Young 1985).

Darwin's metaphor was an apt one, for the artificial generation of domesticated breeds and the natural generation of new species have one fundamental thing in common: both processes depend upon the differential reproductive success of some genetic variants over others in a population of potentially interbreeding organisms. Because of this fundamental similarity, artificial selection can be a useful model of organic evolution. In addition, it can provide evidence concerning the existence of genetic variation in a population with respect to particular phenotypic characteristics.

Consider, for example, the significance of one or two commonplace facts about dogs. Some breeds make good childhood companions, whereas others do not; some breeds make good hunters, whereas others do not; and some breeds make good sheep-dogs, whereas others do not. Most terriers bark a lot, spaniels do so less frequently, and basenjis never seem to do so at all. These and myriad other behavioural differences are the products of domestication; that is, they have all been produced by artificial selection. It follows, therefore, that all of these behavioural differences must either be now or at least once have been subject to genetic variation.

While researching on the behaviour of domesticated dogs, the American ethologists John Scott and John Fuller hybridized cocker spaniels and basenjis in order to discover the genetic differences between them with respect to such characteristics as 'wildness and tameness' of the puppies, 'playful aggressiveness at 13–15 weeks', and 'threshold of stimulation for barking at 11 weeks'. They concluded that the most likely modes of inheritance of breed differences relating to these characteristics were: one dominant gene affecting wildness; two genes with no dominance affecting playful aggressiveness; and two dominant genes affecting the threshold of barking at 11 weeks (Scott and Fuller 1965).

Several important conclusions emerge from this sort of work. First, even very complex and subtle behaviour differences may be influenced by rather simple and straightforward genetic differences. Secondly, at least as important as the genes' role in the determination of specific behaviour differences is their role in the determination of differences in specific learning capabilities. (Many of the most significant differences between dog breeds have to do with what they can or cannot be taught to do; and here, incidentally, is yet another reason why the traditional nature/nurture distinction is so unhelpful.) Thirdly, in domesticated dogs there exist genetic differences affecting almost every aspect of behaviour. Given the extraordinary behavioural diversity of these animals, it is a brave person indeed who will claim with confidence that any given behavioural character in dogs is now and always has been entirely free from genetic influence!

We have seen that the informal (and often quite unconscious) artificial selection by which our domesticated animals have been produced provides us with clues to the relationship between genes and behaviour. In addition, however, artificial selection may be used as a formal experimental technique to very much the same end. For example, in a classic experiment Tryon (1940) selected for maze-running ability in laboratory rats. Having tested an initial population for speed of learning a standard test maze, he chose individuals from both extremes of the resulting behavioural distribution and allowed these to become the ancestors of two separate lineages. Extremely rapid learners were mated with one another, as were extremely slow learners; and, over a number of generations, the two lineages were steadily selected in opposite directions. The result was that they came to possess almost completely non-overlapping learning speed distributions, and Tryon termed the members of each lineage 'bright' and 'dull' to indicate the difference. Using similar techniques, it has proved possible to manipulate many other behavioural characters in rodents, including various measures of 'emotionality' and aggression.

It is often said that success in artificial selection experiments such as these demonstrates the existence of 'a gene for X', where X is, for example, 'brightness' or 'dullness'. This, however, is a very misleading shorthand. It misleads us, first, by suggesting that we have identified a specific genetic influence responsible for the selection effect; whereas in reality all that we have identified is the existence of some genetic influence or other, which may be one gene, several independent genes, or several interacting genes. Of course, as we have already seen from the work of Scott and Fuller, it is sometimes possible to perform different sorts of experiments to determine how many genes may be involved in a given behavioural effect. For example, the situation may be greatly simplified by studying known single-gene effects. Albinism in mice is such an effect, and in one experiment albino males achieved greater mating success than black agouti males, apparently on the basis of greater success in male–male aggressive encounters (Levine 1958). Here, then, we appear to have stronger support for the idea of 'a gene for aggression'.

Yet this is still a seriously misleading shorthand. For it implies, secondly, that we have correctly identified the appropriate behavioural capability – 'brightness' or 'dullness' in the case of Tryon's rats, and 'intermale aggression' in the case of Levine's mice; whereas in reality we cannot be sure that this is so. In the case of Tryon's rats, for example, 'bright' individuals performed better than 'dull' ones only on the particular maze used in the selection experiment; tested on a different maze requiring the use of different cues, the two groups' speeds were the same (Searle 1949). In other words, although it may have been intended to select for general problem-solving ability, Tryon's experiment appears to have selected for a far more specific character that hardly merits the label 'brightness'. The same problem arises with Levine's study of albino mice, incidentally, where the particular reason for the albino males' greater mating success is far from clear.

This sort of difficulty arises very commonly in the genetics of behaviour, and it is related to the third and most serious of all problems with the shorthand phrase 'a gene for X', which is that this phrase misleads us by appearing to specify the developmental relationship between a gene and a behavioural character in a single individual. The phrase 'a gene for X' suggests that the gene or genes in question have a direct and determining relationship with behaviour X; whereas, in reality, all that they have a direct and determining relationship with is an observed difference between X and some other specified behavioural state, in a given developmental and environmental context, and all other things (random or stochastic factors included) being equal. Returning to Tryon's rats once again, we may note that although the 'maze-bright' and 'maze-dull' strains showed large differences in performance in the standard test maze when they were raised in ordinary conditions, these differences disappeared completely when both strains were raised either in a specially restricted or in a specially enriched environment. In other words, the behaviour–genetic difference between the strains was not only maze-specific; it was also specific to the environment in which the rats developed.

The fact that in many animal populations there is genetic variation for a wide range of behavioural characters is undoubtedly important. Not only does it allow us to rationalize and systematize our animal husbandry, but also, as Darwin first clearly realized, it provides us with at least a qualitative justification for adopting an evolutionary approach to behaviour. However, it is essential that this fact be held apart from the mistaken idea that it alone tells us anything one way or the other about the mechanisms or development of behaviour, let alone anything about how behaviour can or should be modified during an individual lifetime. It is useful to know that horses can be bred to be more or less easy to handle; but if we have charge of an individual male foal, we will be well advised to move on pretty quickly from questions about its pedigree to decisions about how it is to be treated and handled in the light of whatever else we may be fortunate enough to know about its probable development under a variety of physical and social regimes.

Sex and aggression

As we have seen, castration is an important technique in the management of male horses. Gelding has its origins in the common observation that stallions are generally more difficult to handle (harder to control, quicker-tempered, more prone to fight one another, etc.) than are mares.

Moreover, it isn't just stallions that are like this; the males of many domesticated animals are in these senses more aggressive than are females; and the same applies to a large number of species in the wild.

Perhaps because in stock management sterilization is far more commonly practised upon males than females (and obviously this fact is not entirely to do with the management of aggression), and perhaps because in Western culture men are commonly regarded as the aggressive sex, many people have come to believe that aggression is a male characteristic only. This is quite wrong. In recent years, biologists have come to pay increasing attention to aggressive behaviour in females (see, for example, Benton, Brain, and Haug 1986); and it has been shown that in many situations (e.g., when it comes to the defence of young) females may be more aggressive than males.

Nevertheless, it remains true that males and females within a single species very often display distinctly different patterns of aggressive behaviour. Such differences are commonly attributed to the influence of the sex hormones. (The 'male hormones', known generically as the androgens (e.g., testosterone) and the 'female hormones', known generically as the oestrogens (e.g., oestrogen) and the progestogens (e.g., progesterone) are actually found in both males and females: the difference between typical males and females in most species is in the relative amounts of these different hormones circulating in the bloodstream.) The question we must ask, therefore, is this: what is the relationship between sex hormones and aggressive behaviour?

The laboratory rat *Rattus norvegicus* is to physiological psychology what the bacterium *Escherichia coli* is to biochemistry and the fruit fly *Drosophila melanogaster* is to classical genetics. As a result of intensive study over many years, we now understand more about the mechanisms subserving the behaviour of the rat than we do about those of any other species, including *Homo sapiens*. This knowledge is obviously very useful, but it does have its dangers. The most obvious among these is that, for want of direct information on other species, we may be tempted to borrow data and conclusions relating to the rat rather too freely. The trouble is that what is true of rats may or may not be true of rattlesnakes and raccoons, let alone of human beings; and the only way to be sure one way or the other is to perform independent studies of the particular species in which we happen to be interested.

The above qualification is important because a great deal of what is known about the relationship between sex hormones and aggression has been derived from work done on rats. In the laboratory, fights between adult male rats occur more commonly than do fights between adult females; and when a male and a non-oestrous female are put together, the male will be dominant. (The situation is greatly complicated when the female enters oestrus, because at this time virtually all social interactions revolve around courtship and mating. Although there may be aggressive aspects to these social interactions, most researchers choose not to analyse them in terms of dominance and subordination.) These well-known facts are usually summed up by stating that male rats are more aggressive than females.

Early work on the physiology of sex-specific behaviour in the rat generated a comparatively straightforward story concerning the part played by the sex hormones. This story may be summarized as follows. In normal genetic males, androgens are produced by the testes in physiologically significant amounts not only as animals approach sexual maturity but also early on in development, during the first week of life (rats are born at a very early stage of development; humans at an equivalent stage would still have many weeks of uterine existence ahead of them). It appears that the early testicular androgens are responsible for physical changes in both the bodies and the brains of males. The external genitalia are directed along a male pathway, and the brain is directed to respond to raised androgen levels in later life with increased amounts of aggressive behaviour – the so-called 'male response'.

In normal genetic females, on the other hand, the absence of testicular androgens early in life leads to the development of the body and brain in a different direction. The external genitalia are directed along a female pathway; and the brain is directed towards the cyclical activity that is the basis of the sexual physiology of the female rat. Moreover, in adult life the female rat will respond to raised levels of female sex hormones with sexually receptive and submissive behaviour – the so-called 'female response' (Archer 1975, 1976; Olioff and Stewart 1978).

Recent studies have refined the rather crude 'on–off switch' idea inherent in this basic story. For example, on the basis of experiments with neonatally castrated males and neonatally androgenized females, as well as normal individuals, van de Poll, Swanson, and van Oyen (1981) have suggested that both androgens and oestrogens may be important in the activation and organization of aggression in the rat. Their results are a mixture of the expected and the unexpected. For example, they find that both normal adult males and adult females that have been androgenized neonatally respond to testosterone with significant increases in aggressiveness towards either a male or a female opponent (the so-called 'male response').

What is more surprising, however, is that both classes of adults respond to oestrogen in exactly the same way. Moreover, both normal adult females and adult males that have been castrated at birth may respond to testosterone alone with a supposedly 'male response', even though this response is supposedly dependent upon neonatal androgenization of the brain, whereas they may respond to a combination of testosterone and oestrogen with a supposedly 'female response'. This 'female response' is also seen in normal adult males and adult females that have been androgenized neonatally when they are treated with physiologically supernormal levels of oestrogen; but it is not seen in these animals when they are treated with testosterone at any level, normal or supernormal.

These less-than-straightforward findings appear to hold for mice as well as rats, although the strains show considerable differences. In golden hamsters, however – and just in case we should be tempted to think that the interrelationships between sex chromosomes, sex hormones, and aggressive behaviour are written in tablets of stone – things are quite different. For one thing, in the laboratory the aggression between female golden hamsters equals or exceeds intermale aggression; a non-oestrous female will attack and successfully drive off an approaching male. In other words, using the same shorthand as was applied to the rat, the golden hamster females are generally more aggressive than are males.

The physiological basis for this behaviour is at least partly understood. In golden hamsters, both castration and ovariectomy produce significant decreases in levels of aggression. If castrated adult males are given either androgens or oestrogens, a normal aggressive response is obtained. However, this is true only so long as the opponent eliciting the aggression is a normal male, or at least an animal that has itself been treated with androgens! On the female side, neither androgens nor oestrogens are effective in inducing normal levels of aggression in ovariectomized females. This, it would appear, is because it is the progestogens that exert the most significant effects on aggression in hamsters. Administered to either a male or a female, progesterone causes both a sharp increase in aggressive behaviour on the part of the treated subject and a sharp decrease in attacks upon the subject from a non-treated male opponent. This last result may explain why non-oestrous female hamsters, which have high levels of progesterone circulating in the blood, are dominant in aggressive encounters with males.

The only simple conclusion that may safely be drawn from these results is that the relationship between chromosomes, sex hormones, and aggression is extremely complex. Not only may sex hormones have different effects on opposite-sex members of the same species, but also they may have different effects on same-sex members of different species. Sex hormones may interact with one another, and the same combination of hormones may have different effects on different individuals and different effects on the same individual at different times. The task of putting all these possibilities together into a single model is, to say the least, somewhat daunting.

One obvious but frequently neglected reason why the relationship between sex hormones and aggression is so complex is that the two variables in question are but part of an altogether larger interactive system comprising not only the fluctuating internal physiological states and behaviour of one individual but also those of one or more potential opponents. In this situation, naively reductionist or single-cause explanations ('it all depends on the hormones ...', 'it all depends on learning ...', etc.) cannot possibly suffice. In many situations changes in the levels of circulating hormones may be as much the consequence as the cause of changes in observed behaviour. Thus, adrenalin levels may rise after the initiation of a fight; and testosterone levels may change in response to a wide variety of factors, from the completion of copulation to the removal of a dominant rival.

What must be involved in each individual is a complex interplay between endogenous processes, including hormones, behavioural outputs, and sensory inputs from an environment that is continually changing in ways only some of which are independent of the individual's own activity. A great deal has been learnt in recent years about various fragments of this interactive system; but in the absence of a coherent view of how these all fit together, it is important to resist the temptation to make one or another of the parts stand in place of the whole. There can be no doubt that sex hormones have an important part to play in the modulation of much aggressive behaviour; but there can be no doubt, either, that this role is both a flexible and a subtle one, and that there are other actors on the stage as well.

Socialization and aggression

The third principle that governs much animal management practice is the conviction that early learning experiences may shape subsequent behaviour. The child, as we say, is father to the man; or returning to our original example, the foal is father to the horse. Obviously, biological study of animal behaviour has as one of its major tasks the clarification of the role of learning in the development of behaviour. Yet this task is far from easy, especially in view of the sharp distinction that Lorenzian ethologists have tended to make in the past between genetic and environmental influences on behaviour. It is worth looking more closely at the Lorenzians' approach to this subject, as it influences the way we tend to think about learning and aggression even today.

Modern ethological studies of animal behaviour have their origins in the work of both Lorenz and Tinbergen in Germany and the Netherlands in the late-1930s. For Lorenz, the dominant theoretician throughout this period, what made ethology different from other approaches to animal behaviour was its generally biological orientation, and in particular its stress upon the role of internal or 'innate' factors in the genesis of behaviour. In his early programmatic writings, Lorenz was at pains to distinguish the nascent field of ethology from all other schools of behavioural science, and particularly from American behaviourism. Where, according to Lorenz, behaviourism portrayed animals as open learning machines governed by patterns of external stimuli (rewards and punishments), ethology portrayed them as more-or-less closed learning machines driven by patterns of internal biological stimuli ('instincts' or 'innate drives'; Lorenz 1971). For Lorenz, as for virtually all ethologists then and now, it made no sense whatever to think of newborn animals as empty vessels waiting to be filled with information by passive learning experiences. Rather, animals were to be seen as coming into the world equipped by evolution with certain expectancies and dispositions, such that even the earliest learning experiences were both active and selective.

It was in his studies of 'imprinting' (German: *Prägung*) that Lorenz did most to develop an ethological model of learning. Imprinting was the name that had been given by Lorenz's mentor Oskar Heinroth to the tendency of newly hatched chicks to become attached to a 'mother object'. In a series of famous experiments with hand-reared goslings, Lorenz investigated this phenomenon in some detail. He showed that his goslings could become permanently attached to an adult bird of the wrong species, or even to himself. In fact, just as long as the chicks were kept apart from their true mothers and exposed to an alternative mother object during a brief 'critical period' after hatching, unique and long-lasting bonds could be formed to almost anything. It was as if the goslings were born expecting to encounter their mother and predisposed to follow her through thick and thin.

Imprinting was a concept of great importance in the early days of ethology precisely because it offered a new way of understanding the relationship between internal (innate or instinctive) and external (environmental or learning) factors in the development of behaviour. Imprinting was seen as showing that animals were predisposed towards learning particular things; that is, they were biased towards some features of their environment, and away from others. On this basis, Lorenz formulated a view of behaviour development as involving the 'intercalation' of instinct and learning (Lorenz 1971).

The term intercalation is significant here. Originally, it referred to the insertion of extra days into the calendar year to make it equal to the solar year. In the same way, Lorenz viewed learning as the insertion of particular items of information from the environment into a sequence of behaviour development laid down in advance by the genes. That a gosling had a mother, and that it should form a specific and long-lasting bond with her, were, so-to-speak, biologically preordained; all that learning did was to supply at the appropriate point the missing item of information: 'your mother is object X'. Lorenz once captured the spirit of this view by suggesting that animals possess an 'innate school-marm' directing what they are to learn!

It was out of this general view of behaviour that classical ethology fashioned the concept of 'developmentally scheduled sensitivities' (Hess 1973). Having long since abandoned what they took to be the 'animal as empty vessel' view of behaviourism, many ethologists opted for a theory of developmental stages, each with its particular 'window(s)' on the external world. At any particular stage, a learning window was regarded as opening for a predetermined interval of time (in the case of imprinting, this was the 'critical period' during which attachment to a mother object was possible). While the window was open, a specific stimulus caused a specific learnt response; but once the window was closed, the same stimulus was ineffective. Implicit in this view was the notion that in order for an animal to behave 'appropriately' in adult life, it was necessary that the correct stimuli should have entered through each window in the brief interval of time during which it was open.

As this brief account is intended to suggest, early imprinting researchers tended to regard developmental windows as both extremely indiscriminate as regards what they let through and extremely inflexible as regards the influence of what went through on subsequent behaviour. A duckling imprinted on a hen during its critical period for the development of the following response, for example, was seen as acquiring not only a rigid attachment to the hen as its mother object but also a rigid sexual preference for other hens on reaching maturity.

More recent work has shown that this is altogether too simple a picture. In some cases, the window appears to be left slightly open far beyond what had been regarded as the critical period; and in others there appears to be a second window for the development of sexual preferences. Moreover, early attachments and preferences may be modifiable on occasions when more 'appropriate' partners are introduced (Hess 1973). If behaviour development involves an internal calendar at all, it is a good deal more complex and a good deal more subtle than the calendars we use to keep track of the passing years.

For all its obvious simplicity, the metaphor of developmental windows has been and continues to be useful. For one thing, it enables us to incorporate learning into evolutionary explanations of behaviour. Windows themselves, their degrees of selectivity, and the time intervals during which they are open are all potential variables that may be influenced by natural selection. Moreover, by considering the habits and habitats of different animals, one can formulate sensible hypotheses about the evolution of developmentally scheduled sensitivities.

For example, in the case of so-called precocial animals that must move around with their parents immediately after birth (such as many ducks), it is clearly important that the major features and figures within the environment be learned very rapidly; here, therefore, we may expect to find imprinting. In the case of so-called altricial animals that are physically confined to a nest for long periods after birth (such as many songbirds), on the other hand, it is not particularly important that the young be able to identify objects and individuals in this way; and here, imprinting may not be needed at all.

A mammalian analogue of the imprinting studies on birds is, once again, the work of John Scott; but this time, his work not on the behaviour genetics of domesticated dogs but rather on their social development. Scott divides the developmental life of a dog into six periods: neonatal, transition, socialization, juvenile, pubertal, and parental. Each period occupies a specific interval of time and is characterized by the appearance of specific types of behaviour. Furthermore, during each period the developing puppy is receptive to particular sorts of stimuli. Here we may invoke the window concept again, but we must be careful to use it in a rather refined way. Scott's dogs differ individually and by breed. They have many windows, more than one of which may be open at any one time; and rather than opening and closing in an all-or-nothing fashion, these windows operate smoothly and gradually on well-oiled hinges.

The period of socialization is one of the most important stages in terms of its influence on adult behaviour. Experiences that occur or fail to occur at this stage can have a lasting effect. Consider, for example, the development of aggressive behaviour. Scott reports a definite genetic component in aggression differences between breeds. However, the aggressiveness of any particular dog can be greatly affected by socialization experiences, to the point where breed differences may be abolished or even reversed. Thus, fox terriers are 'by nature' more aggressive than beagles. Yet your adult male terrier may be much less inclined to bite and snap at visitors than your neighbour's adult male beagle. It may be, for example, that you brought your dog into your household as a six-week-old pup, that you and your children lavished it with attention, and that when it was old enough you gave it a thorough course of obedience classes. On the other hand, it may be that your neighbour received his beagle when it was already a year old, and that for most of this year the dog had been kept alone at a large breeding kennel, receiving very little contact with other dogs or humans. Granted, this is a somewhat extreme hypothetical example, but it does serve to illustrate the way in which socialization can influence the development of aggressive behaviour in dogs.

It has long been assumed that there is more to be learnt about human social development from our closest relatives the monkeys and apes than there is from other mammals. The best studied of all non-human primates, at least in the laboratory, is the rhesus monkey (*Macaca mulatta*). Under normal circumstances, a newborn rhesus monkey spends its first week of life clinging closely to its mother. At this stage, it is relatively helpless and utterly dependent upon its mother for food, warmth, and protection. As it grows older, however, the baby monkey gradually becomes less passive. It begins to leave its mother and interact with other monkeys for increasingly longer periods of time, returning to her for food and (we may presume) for comfort and confidence. At this stage, the similarities between baby rhesus monkeys and toddlers in a playgroup are striking to even the most strictly non-anthropomorphic observer.

Just now important is the mother to normal social development among primates? This question had intrigued zoo-keepers for decades before properly controlled experiments were begun in the 1960s in an attempt to answer it scientifically. The most widely known studies were conducted by Harry Harlow and his co-workers at the University of Wisconsin (Harlow and Harlow 1965), who raised rhesus monkeys with mother surrogates consisting of cloth-covered wire frames with attached nursing bottles. Monkeys kept under such conditions of extreme isolation for their first year of life developed severe and permanent behavioural disabilities. Introduced into a social group, they initially huddled in corners, sucked their fingers and toes, hugged themselves tightly, and were extremely fearful; and even after they had become more accustomed to their new social surroundings, other abnormalities continued to appear. These included variant sexual and maternal behaviour, and hyperaggressivity in interactions with peers.

If the period of rearing in isolation was shortened to six months, the permanency of some aberrant behaviour patterns was reduced; but monkeys reared in this way still failed to mature into socially normal adults. Isolation for only the first three months of life, however, seemed to produce no lasting effects. Young monkeys treated this way exhibited distress and abnormal behaviour at first encountering other animals, but they were able to overcome their early disabilities and developed normally thereafter.

These first experiments suggested that socialization is a continuous process, and that the timing of events during normal social development is especially significant. However, rearing a monkey in complete isolation is a very violent departure from nature, and it sheds little light on the nature of the social relationships that are essential to normal development. Harlow's group turned their attention to this issue by raising newborn rhesus monkeys in a variety of specific social settings and studying the results in later life. For example, they found that individuals raised with their mother alone for the first four years of life tended to become unaffectionate, unsocial, and hyperaggressive adults. By contrast, individuals raised in peer groups without a mother tended to develop extremely close social contacts with one another, often clinging together in a tight bunch; and, given time, they were able to develop into relatively normally functioning adults.

On the basis of these and similar results it has been widely concluded that interactions with peers are more important to normal social development (in terms of affectionate relationships, aggressiveness, communication skills, etc.) than are interactions with a mother. However, this is somewhat simplistic. There is no question that in the case both of rhesus monkeys and of many other primate species, the mother's role extends far beyond mere nourishment and physical protection. Indeed, she is often indirectly responsible for the peer-group contacts that her offspring make, providing the security upon which they build their first adventures into the wider social world, and 'rescuing' them as and when adventure starts to turn into misadventure. As we might have expected, there are significant individual differences in the mother–infant relationship within the species. Some mothers, for example, appear to provide better socialization for their offspring than others do. Both a very fearful, timid mother and a very protective, assertive one may prevent their babies from making effective contact with peers; and as we have seen, this can have permanently damaging results.

What, then, of the specific effects of early social experience upon the development of aggressive behaviour? Here, it is difficult to generalize. In some primate species, early social isolation produces adults that tend to be less aggressive than normal (often because they are simply less active and reactive all round). In others, as we have seen with rhesus monkeys, such isolation produces the opposite effect, with socially deprived adults showing increased aggression both towards peers and (in the case of females) towards their own offspring. Here, as before, both the precise nature of the effects produced and their permanence depend upon a variety of factors: the degree of social isolation suffered, the age at which it begins, how long it endures, and so on.

The significance of these effects is, however, far from clear. In general, isolation-induced aggression tends to be grossly maladaptive; that is, it does not enhance but rather seriously detracts from the actor's reproductive success. The most obvious example under this heading is a mother attacking her own offspring, but there are many others. Such obviously non-functional aggression may with some justice be labelled 'pathological', and it is an open question how much it tells us about the obviously functional aggression that may be studied in undisturbed environments. To the extent that they produce such gross behavioural pathologies as maternal infanticide (and always assuming that we are not witnessing one of natural selection's more bizarre manifestations; see Hrdy 1977, and Hausfater and Hrdy 1984), social-isolation experiments may be of limited relevance to the understanding of 'natural' behaviour.

The substantial literature on the development of social behaviour in non-human primates appears to yield at least three general conclusions: first, virtually all species of higher primates appear to need extensive 'schooling' for adult life during infancy; secondly, early social contacts play a vital part in this 'schooling', providing opportunities both for psychological comfort and support and for the acquisition of social skills through direct imitation and trial-and-error learning; and, thirdly, there is often more than one developmental pathway to the evolutionary goal of reproductively successful adult social behaviour, such that social deprivation in one direction may, if not too severe, be compensated by social experiences in another.

To go much beyond these generalizations, it is necessary to deal directly with the particular species in which we happen to be interested; and in the case of our own species, this is merely another way of saying that primatology must give way to developmental psychology and sociology.

The path from animals to humans

It is a sobering fact that horse breeders and horse trainers are far more skilled than ethologists at manipulating and moulding the behaviour of their animals. In the same way, parents are far better than psychologists at predicting the behaviour of children. For the most part, our informal or tacit knowledge of the development of social behaviour still far exceeds our formal or explicit knowledge; and, as scientists, we are in the all-too-familiar position of trying to grasp more clearly the full implications of things that we have known, or half-known, all along. This is no reason for despondency, but it does serve to indicate how far we have come in our understanding of behaviour development, compared with how far there is still to go.

Human behaviour is, of course, perfectly fair game for ethological investigation. However, it is important to remember that, if it is human behaviour we want to understand, it is human beings we had better study; making use of animal data and generalizing them to cover our own species simply will not do. This is not only or even primarily because humans possess unique characteristics that make their behaviour qualitatively different from that of other animals (though they do, and it is), but also because when it comes to something as complex and variable as social behaviour every species deserves individual study.

As we have seen in this chapter, it is a long way from imprinting in goslings to mother–infant relationships in rhesus monkeys. It is even further from either of these to interactions within the human family. Considering how much we already know about the development of social behaviour in a large number of other species, and in particular about the major differences that exist both within and between them, it should be clear that sound generalizations embracing many or even all animal species are few and far between. Aggressive behaviour is not a single or a simple thing (indeed, it is not a thing at all); and it is not the outcome of a single or a simple developmental process in all animals, or even in all primates. Thus, we should beware of the easy transposition of conclusions concerning aggressive behaviour from other species – including even such comparatively close relatives as the great apes – to ourselves.

CHAPTER SIX

As the twig is bent: Themes in human development

A lame metaphor

As the twig is bent, so grows the tree. Or does it? If a large limb falls on a small sapling, the sapling may be nearly flattened; but it may eventually recover, turning its growing point to the sky and continuing to seek the sun. Here, bending does not determine growth but is compensated for by it. Again, trees on the coast demonstrate 'wind shear', a growth form leaning away from the prevailing wind; but this is not because twigs that are persistently bent by the wind come to grow in that direction. The actual mechanism is less obvious. Salt spray continually driving against coastal trees produces dehydration, and this stunts the growth of buds and shoots on the windward side, while those on the relatively sheltered leeward side grow normally. The wind's effect is thus indirect, and bending has nothing to do with it.

The bent twig is a poor parable for plant growth, and it is no better as a model of human social development. Countless research hours have been devoted to different parental practices and their effects on children's subsequent behaviour. Summing up the outcome of this effort in a single sentence, it may be said that there are significant effects, but that these are rarely simple and never straightforward; what parents do makes a difference, but not in any very direct or easily predictable way. Severe punishment, for example, may cause one child to obey, another to rebel, and a third simply to withdraw. This, presumably, is because such variables as the temperament of the child, the quality of the parent–child relationship, the way that both parent and child have come to view the legitimacy of particular acts, and factors outside the parent–child relationship may all influence the outcome.

Developmental biology and psychology are at least as constrained by popular preconceptions as any other branch of the behavioural sciences. Here, too, the nature/nurture distinction has influenced a great deal of research. Dominating the study of behaviour development until comparatively recently have been the twin shibboleths of nativism and behaviourism, each representing a commitment to either nature or nurture as the crucial influence. In this chapter, we shall take a fresh look at the development of human aggression, unencumbered (so far as is possible) by the nature/nurture distinction. Our aim will be, not to construct a detailed model of the development of human aggression, but rather to establish what such a model will have to be like if it is to do justice to the complexity and the subtlety of the interactions that generate human conflict.

Before beginning this task, one further caution is in order. Precisely because of the nature of social development, studies in this area are inevitably constrained not only by popular cultural conceptions of human nature but also by the kinds of settings in which research is conducted. Much of the available literature on our subject is painfully parochial; not only does the vast bulk of it deal with children growing up in Western industrial societies, but also most of it is based on work with children growing up within very particular (relatively wealthy, so-called 'middle class') families. In years to come, when more adequate comparative data have been collected, it may be that this literature will be seen as far more informative about the specific cultures on which it is based than it is about general developmental processes common across cultures. Only time, of course, will tell.

Studying social development

At the beginning of our inquiry, it may be useful to summarize one or two recent trends in the psychological study of social development. Four broad areas of interest may be discerned. First, it has been shown that children do show marked individual differences in temperament or 'behavioural style' from birth (for reviews, see Buss and Plomin 1975; Thomas and Chess 1977). Obviously, such differences may influence the social environments in which children grow up. A very active or energetic child will set a different tone for social interactions than will a very passive or a lethargic one; and others, finding that they prefer interacting with a child who is more (or less) active, may respond accordingly. Again, a more active child may well select livelier friends and playmates than a less active one. In such ways, the child's temperament may modify its social environment; and this environment may in turn act back upon temperament – more active children may attract more attention, which may in turn foster the disposition towards further activity, and so on.

A second area of interest has been in the quality of the parent–child relationship, which has come increasingly to be seen as incapable of reduction to simple-minded, one-way processes. For example, several studies have shown a correlation between parental rejection and high levels of aggression in children (Feshbach 1970). This correlation might be explained in several different ways: (1) rejecting parents might cause frustration and anxiety in their children, which in turn might cause aggressive behaviour; (2) overly aggressive children might elicit rejecting behaviour from their parents; or (3) elements of (1) and (2) might both be involved within a progressively more antagonistic relationship. Clearly, something other than mere correlation is needed to distinguish between these hypotheses; but at first glance, most psychologists today would probably be inclined to opt for (3). The argument here would be that the parent–child relationship is inherently reciprocal, with each side continually shaping and being shaped by the other.

Thirdly, there has been growing interest in the role of cognitive factors in human social development. Following in the pioneering footsteps of Jean Piaget (see, for example, Piaget and Inhelder 1969), psychologists have attempted to follow the path along which children's cognitive capabilities travel from birth to maturity. Thus, the recognition of others as separate from oneself occurs during the first year of life; an understanding of rules may begin around the age of 3–5; the attribution of intentions to others does not occur until after the age of 6 or 7; and self-reflective role-playing does not generally appear until around the age of 8–10. A sense of moral obligation is the trickiest of all mental attributes to tie to age; indeed, in some cases it appears never to emerge at all! Such abilities as these arise (or not, as the case may be) within a particular developmental environment; and they contribute importantly to the determination of social behaviour in that environment.

This is most easily seen if we consider the importance of the concept of legitimacy in the genesis of aggressive behaviour. Consider a simple example. Two customers enter into separate agreements with a watchmaker for the repair of their watches within a week. Returning at the end of the week, one of them is told rather curtly that his watch is not ready, because the watchmaker has been watching Wimbledon on TV; whereas the other is told rather apologetically that her watch is not ready, because there has been unexpected illness in the watchmaker's family. The first customer responds aggressively, but the second does not. (This sort of situation has been engineered experimentally, with just these results.) Now the crucial difference between these two cases is surely that in the one the watchmaker's excuse is regarded as illegitimate, whereas in the other it is regarded as legitimate. This distinction depends upon a quite sophisticated understanding of intention, obligation, and the morality of conduct; and such capabilities emerge only very gradually during development.

Fourth and last, the investigation of children's social development has widened beyond the mother–child dyad to embrace both the study of interactions in whole families and the relationship between such interactions and what goes on outside the home. For example, in a series of studies, Robert Hinde and his co-workers have explored the relationship between children's social interactions within the family and their behaviour in day nurseries. Building on the foundation of earlier work with rhesus monkeys, which pointed to the importance of a social 'nexus' in which there is interaction between social interactions, Hinde (1974) is attempting to identify significant correlations within the wider social nexus of human infants.

Seen as a nexus of social interactions, development is an enormously complex process; but techniques such as multivariate analysis allow for the identification of constellations of characteristics that may together be far better predictors of future outcomes than are single factors. For example, one study evaluated the home situations of a group of boys aged between 5 and 13 (McCord 1979). A cluster of variables – for example, the parental characteristics parent aggressiveness, paternal deviance, and mother's lack of self-confidence, and child-rearing variables such as supervision, parental conflict, and maternal affection – correctly predicted 80 per cent of adult criminality in this group, as measured by court records 30 years later.

The widening of the focus of recent research on social development represents a recognition by psychologists of the subtlety of child development. The assumption that a few environmental factors could determine the overall direction of growth throughout childhood ('As the twig is bent . . .') has given way to a view of development in which there is continuous interaction among multiple factors, prominent among which are the child's own personality and its unfolding social awareness. In Chapter 4, we saw that the subjective and intersubjective meaning of events plays a crucial part in the interpretation of different cultures; exactly the same thing is true of the interpretation of different individuals' growth and development.

Some useful concepts

The concept of socialization is central to the study of social development. Socialization is the name given to the processes by which children are constructed by and in turn help to construct their social world. Socialization always proceeds within a pre-existing culture, and it entails the acquisition of the shared beliefs, perceptions, and symbols that together define social reality within that culture. This, as we have already suggested, is an active process; the child attends selectively to its environment, building into its model of reality some things at the same time that it disregards others. The child's response to external events is a function of its personal identity at any given moment in time; and this personal identity must be seen as the product of many variables, including both genetic and environmental (including cultural) factors interacting within an individual life history.

Based upon so many variables, personal identity may take many particular forms; but it may not take an infinite number of them. The biological and cultural factors that together contribute to the child's construction of its social world are very variable, but they are not endlessly so. This is only another way of saying that the range of possible personal identities among humankind is somewhat smaller than the range of theoretically conceivable personal identities in worlds non-human or inhuman - we are not free, presumably, to be angels (i.e., aetherial and aerial personal beings with exclusively virtuous habits; but see C.S. Lewis's classic *Screwtape Letters* (1942) for a somewhat different view). Of course, it may be that certain rather more mundane human social forms are 'out of bounds' as well; but in order to know this we should need a comprehensive knowledge of all relevant gene-gene and gene-environment interactions for all relevant human genotypes in all relevant physical and social environments - a requirement so far from being realized today that we are well advised to avoid the whole notion of 'limits' as being, in the worst sense of the term, of 'academic interest' only (Kitcher 1985).

A great deal of this book is devoted to the attempt to shed older styles of thought based on the false dichotomy between genetic and environmental determinism. Helpful in this task is the concept of 'goodness of fit' between organism and environment. Goodness of fit occurs when the characteristics and demands of an organism's environment are in accord with that organism's capabilities and dispositions. A gorilla in its native forest shows such goodness of fit; a gorilla in a typical zoo, unfortunately, does not. When there is good fit, optimal growth and development are possible. Where there is poor fit, and the dissonance is not too great, individuals may be able to compensate; but extreme dissonance may result in severe developmental distortions. The late 'Guy', for many years Britain's best-known captive gorilla, appears to have been unable to compensate for the poverty of his social environment at the London Zoo. Had he been human, he might have spent much of his adult life in a different sort of institution, where doctors and warders rather than holidaymakers and schoolchildren would have stared through bars into his troubled eyes.

The major advantage of the concept of goodness of fit is that it helps to get us away from the 'As the twig is bent . . .' mode of thought by defining development in terms of a reciprocal relationship (goodness of fit may change when any or all of the following things change: the temperamental or other 'endogenous' characteristics of the individual; the subjective characteristics of the individual, including his or her self-conscious attitudes and beliefs; the number, nature, dispositions of, or interactions with and between other individuals in the social environment; and, last but not necessarily least, the non-social setting). The major disadvantage of the concept, however, is that it is inevitably value-laden. To say that there is goodness of fit between organism and environment is to say that things are as they should be; and we should be careful not to forget that judgements on this last point are necessarily dependent upon a prior (though not necessarily moral) evaluative stance.

Aggression as a developmental construct

'Aggression' is one of the many social constructs which children may form as they grow up. (We have all grown up, but it is worth recalling that none of us is finished with the process yet.) Children learn what anger is, how they may be angry, and when their anger may be displayed; they learn how, when, and why others may act aggressively; and they learn to cope with their own and other people's aggression. Youngsters everywhere soon pick up a working knowledge of what they and others can or cannot get away with; they rapidly come to know what is polite or rude, fair or unfair, moral or immoral, and even legal or illegal. 'What' in each of these cases refers not merely to a list of items that happen to fall into a particular category but also, and much more importantly, to the underlying concepts that give that category its cognitive coherence and social meaning.

Though they may or may not learn the word 'aggression', many young children in Western societies soon learn that bullying, threatening, or hitting a schoolmate or sibling is rarely approved of. Parents and teachers usually give reasons for their displeasure, appealing to ideals of fairness, kindness, and consideration; they often encourage empathy ('How would you feel if someone did that to you?'), and they may foster reconciliatory manoeuvres involving bargaining and sharing. But the message that they get across to children is not a simple one. Should a child be 'too passive' it may lose the respect of both peers and adults; and then there may follow encouragement to 'stick up for yourself!'. Some things, children learn, are 'worth fighting for'.

The rules by which we discriminate between those things that ought and those things that ought not to be fought over are often unclear; and sometimes situations arise where a youngster is 'damned if it does and damned if it doesn't'. An Israeli friend recently described to one of us his experience of growing up in a predominantly Jewish quarter of New York under his mother's twin rules – 'be proud you're a Jew', and 'don't get into any trouble'. Faced with the hostile question from a street gang leader, 'Hey, boy, are you a Jew?', and uncertain how best to abide by his mother's somewhat tricky advice, he replied, 'No, I'm a Hebrew', and escaped without a bloody nose. The point here is that children acquire great expertise in judging how to behave. Potential benefits – peer and parental approval, the achievement of practical goals, etc. – are weighed in the balance against potential costs – peer ostracism or ridicule, parental punishment, or even a bloody nose. In this calculation, esteem – the standing that one has in the eyes of others – may be a crucially important variable, particularly for older children and adults (Harré 1979).

The fact that aggression (or some similar term) is widely used across cultures as a convenient construct does not mean that it is necessarily a good guide in the study of the causal processes underlying behaviour. The human ethologist N.G. Blurton Jones has illustrated this last point well in his work on the social behaviour of nursery children. He found that the analytical category 'rough-and-tumble play' was not very closely related to the analytical category 'aggression'. Indeed, comparisons of individual, age, and sex differences in behaviour tended to undermine the category 'aggression' altogether (Blurton Jones 1972). The very broadness and flexibility that serve to make aggression such a convenient label in popular parlance may serve to make it a poor tool for the altogether stricter purposes of science.

Aggression and social development

Infancy

The most important business of infancy appears to be feeding, staying warm and protected, and getting on with the hard work of growing up. Healthy babies are, as we might expect, well equipped for these tasks. In particular, they readily establish bonds with their caretakers, turning their heads towards a voice, following a face with their eyes, crying when things are not as they should be, and (before long) smiling when things are going well. For their part, caretakers appear also to be well equipped for the task of child-rearing. Most adults appear to find infants very appealing, are upset by the sound of a baby in distress, and are pleased by the sight of a baby's smile. It has been claimed that humans are predisposed to find babyish features attractive (Lorenz 1971); and certainly, this entire constellation of parent–infant interactions looks like just the sort of thing one might expect to evolve by natural selection in the interests of greater reproductive success.

We have already noted that children show individual differences in temperament right from birth; that is, even before they have begun to participate in social interactions. It is perfectly possible that some of these initial differences are the result of prenatal environmental differences; but it is also possible that some of them are the result of genetic differences. Hard evidence relating to this latter possibility is notoriously difficult to obtain. As was pointed out in Chapter 5, however, humans have long practised artificial selection of their domesticated animals in order to produce more docile and easily handleable varieties; and such selection demonstrates the existence of genetic variation for these temperamental traits. On the one hand, this does not prove anything one way or the other about our own species; but on the other, there is no particular reason to suppose that we are radically different from other animals in this respect.

The psychiatrists Alexander Thomas and Stella Chess have been conducting longitudinal studies on the development of temperament since the early 1950s. Their sample consists of 133 children from a socially rather homogeneous middle- or upper-middle-class and predominantly Jewish community living in New York. Using direct observation and interviews, Thomas and Chess have been regularly assessing as many different situations as possible with a view to obtaining measurements through time of nine different categories of temperament: activity level; rhythmicity; approach or withdrawal; adaptability; threshold of responsiveness; intensity of reaction; quality of mood; distractability; and attention span and persistence (Thomas and Chess 1977).

Thomas and Chess began their work with the notion that consistency over time was important to the concept of temperament; but when they analysed their data, they found a significant amount of developmental variation. Although some temperamental traits remained reasonably consistent over time, there were others that showed distortion (or even wholesale transformation) in response to a variety of psychological and environmental influences. Thomas and Chess concluded that temperament, like many other psychological characteristics, cannot be expected to show linear continuity over time. They argued that although the process of organism–environment interaction may be predictable to some extent, temperamental and behavioural consistency arises only when a certain sort of fit between organism and environment is maintained.

Early experience and aggression

How does all this relate to aggression? When does aggressive behaviour first occur; what does it look like; and how does it change through time? What temperamental and social factors influence the character, frequency, and intensity of childhood aggression?

No behaviour that can be recognized as an attempt to hurt or injure someone else appears to occur among very young babies. The only even remotely aggressive behaviour discernible at this early stage is full-blooded, red-faced, no-holds-barred yelling. This is sometimes referred to in the literature as 'undirected rage', but in practice it is very difficult to distinguish from general distress. Certainly, young babies lack the cognitive ability and the social awareness necessary for the performance of the kinds of aggressive acts seen in children and adults; and it may be no more than an imposition of adult feelings of irritation or annoyance to describe such behaviour as aggressive.

It is only very gradually that behaviour that may be described as unambiguously aggressive makes its appearance. One- and two-year-olds, for example, may try to grab toys from each other, or to strike each other; they do not, however, appear to try to hurt or to injure each other. Grabbing is not difficult to explain – in one study of 21-month-old playmates, it emerged as a far more successful way of acquiring a toy than actually asking for it (Hay and Ross 1982); but such encounters also have a social significance beyond mere acquisition. Frequently, toys appear to become desirable only when someone else has them, and it is difficult not to accept that personal rivalries and 'petty jealousy' begin as early as this.

It is doubtful if intentionally hurtful action directed at others occurs before the age of two. After this age, children may display 'Fixation, frowning, directed hitting or threats thereof' (Maccoby 1980). Interestingly, the young children who do these things most are in general the more socially competent and sociable individuals. Those who often get into squabbles are also frequently to be found helping or comforting a playmate. Indeed, even at this stage it is still difficult in many cases to distinguish between fighting and playing. Rough-and-tumble play, for example, is a form of activity in which a lot of generally abrasive interactions take place, but clear conflict and lasting alienation rarely occur. This is not to say, however, that more straightforwardly aggressive behaviour is never found. In one study of three- to five-year-olds, there was a recognizable group of boys who were both highly aggressive and not at all sociable (Yarrow and Waxler 1976).

It has been suggested that there is a relationship between aggression and temperament in infancy. Buss and Plomin (1975) believe that early aggressiveness is explained by a combination of high overall activity, high 'emotionality' (meaning ease of arousal, intensity of reaction, and level of affect), and high 'impulsivity'. There is an intriguing sex difference here, with high emotionality in boys being associated with high levels of aggressiveness, but high emotionality in girls being associated with high levels of fearfulness and reduced aggressiveness. Whatever we make of these results, we should bear in mind the work of Thomas and Chess, which suggests that early temperamental characteristics are subject to change over time. Although these two groups of researchers have used slightly different classifications of temperament, their work does seem broadly comparable; we may expect, therefore, that aggressiveness associated with particular early temperaments will display a variety of 'careers' as children mature.

When it comes to the question of the relationship between the quality of early social experience and patterns of aggressiveness later on in childhood or adult life, the situation is far from clear. An association between adult criminality and early social deprivation has been widely noted; and to the extent that adult criminality is associated with violent behaviour, there would appear to be a significant correlation between socialization and aggression in later life. However, it is far from easy to interpret this correlation. Early social deprivation may itself be associated with low economic status, exposure to greater amounts of violence outside the home, and a general environment that affords greater than average opportunities for achieving personal goals by means of aggressive behaviour. These and many other factors need further untangling before we can claim really to understand the relevance of early social experience and subsequent patterns of aggressive behaviour.

Childhood

In general, the usefulness of aggression as a tactic for achieving personal goals declines through the early and middle years of childhood. From preschool years on, there is an overall decline in the frequence of aggressive encounters between children: such aggression as there is tends to be less physical and more verbal; and such physical attacks as do occur tend to be less 'instrumental' (e.g., fights over toys) and more person-directed or 'hostile' (Hartup 1974).

It is not difficult to explain these changes. As children reach school age, they find that while on occasions it may be possible to get what they want by threatening or hurting someone, the drawbacks of such behaviour are increasingly great. Quite apart from the problem of punishment, there are the serious risks of retaliation and the loss of valuable friends. Most of the pressures at this stage are in favour of bargaining and conditional cooperation, as children discover that there are ways of getting what they want that are more effective in the long term than mere bullying or coercion. (For a more systematic treatment of this important subject, see the discussion in Chapter 8 on the evolution of cooperative behaviour.)

These changes are facilitated by a number of interrelated developments. First, there is increasingly good impulse control. Most children over the age of five show rapid improvement in their abilities to stay still for extended periods of time, to think before acting, to accept delays in achieving goals, and generally to tolerate frustration. Secondly, children acquire increasingly impressive communication skills that enable them to resolve conflicts by means of bargaining and cooperation. Also at this stage, and thirdly, comes increasing empathy, or awareness of the feelings of others; and, fourthly, with empathy (especially when it is coupled with frequent admonitions to show respect for others' feelings) may come sympathy, or concern for the feelings of others. It is now, fifthly, that children come to be able to read the intentions of others reasonably well; most children over the age of six, for example, clearly distinguish between those hurtful actions that are accidental and those that are intentional. Sixthly, it is now that children begin to make use of the concept of the legitimacy of other people's actions. The seventh and final point to be made is that after the age of five, children pass through a series of developmental stages in their capacity to make moral judgements (see Piaget 1965, and Kohlberg 1969, 1981). Obviously, these aspects of personal development are closely interwoven, and together they constitute the framework within which new patterns of aggressive behaviour emerge throughout childhood.

Aggression within the family

Parents wear at least four different hats where their children are concerned. First, they are models of adult behaviour. Social-learning theorists have placed great emphasis on children's tendency to imitate others, particularly those in positions of authority (Bandura 1969, 1971). For different reasons, psychoanalytic theorists have stressed the identification of children with the parent of the same sex, together with the internalization of parental values. Whatever the theory, there can be no doubt that parents are important as examples of what to do. Secondly, parents normally act as their children's first partners in social interaction. As the earliest representatives of the social world, parents play an enormously important part in shaping children's early social awareness; and they may, of course, continue to act as central partners and guides for many years. Thirdly, parents have a strong though often subtle role as managers of their children's behaviour: as the setters of the rules governing private conduct, sibling interactions, behaviour outside the home, and so on. Fourthly, parents serve also as teachers, that is they actively direct and shape their children's behaviour, implanting knowledge, inculcating manners, fostering attitudes, and defending values.

The relative importance of these four hats is, of course, almost endlessly debatable. Eleanor Maccoby, for example, has argued that 'the parents' most lasting influence probably comes through establishing modes of interacting with other people and teaching certain modes of adaptation to changing life circumstances' (Maccoby 1980:29); but here science is perhaps a poor guide compared with biography and autobiography, and certainly each parent will have their own distinctive view of what they are up to.

Violence within the home is today the subject of increasing public concern, as well as considerable academic interest. Studies of family violence have shown that there is a close relationship between the way parents settle differences between themselves, the way parents discipline children, and the way children settle differences between themselves (see, for example, Steinmetz 1977; Steinmetz and Straus 1974). Generally speaking, parents who tend to shout at or hit one another tend to shout at or hit their children, who tend in turn to shout at or hit one another. Sibling–sibling aggression occurs more frequently than spouse–spouse or parent–child aggression, whereas the damage done by children is less.

The work of G.R. Patterson provides an unusually detailed picture of some of the family interaction patterns that can occur. One study compared a group of socially aggressive boys (identified as 'out of control' by their families, their school authorities, or the courts) with a group of normal boys matched for age and social background (Patterson 1982). In-home observations were made on each family member and behaviour was coded every five seconds. Interactions in the families of out-of-control boys took the form of long chains of coercion and counter-coercion between family members. Teasing, threatening, or whining from one individual would bring retaliation from another, which in turn would elicit a fresh round of acrimonious exchanges. Punishment by parents occurred more frequently in the families of the aggressive boys, but it often failed to put a stop to the undesirable behaviour. In fact, it often resulted in an escalation of the conflict. By contrast, the parents in the control families were more likely to ignore or tolerate aversive behaviour for a while, but when they finally acted the undesirable behaviour stopped.

The picture of the problem families that emerges from Patterson's study is one of parents who are punitive at the same time that they are essentially uninvolved. All the members of the problem families tended to avoid one another. They did not often sit down together to talk things over, and joint problem-solving was not a part of their daily experience. Patterson suggests that the parents of the aggressive boys responded to their children's aversive behaviour as if they were children themselves, getting drawn into the bickering and losing sight of the issue that had started the conflict in the first place. These parents provided neither the example nor the training in cooperative and sympathetic social interaction that might have allowed the rest of the family to find non-aggressive ways of working out their differences.

If this study is any guide, the path to well-adjusted children is one along which parents remain committed to their children's welfare and responsive to their needs. Parents should notice what their children are doing, and be prepared to respond consistently, firmly, and (where possible) non-violently. In addition to modelling and teaching positive skills and values such as cooperation and respect for others, parents should encourage family members to talk and listen to one another a great deal, since it is in the process of mutual exchange that such skills and values are most easily and rapidly acquired.

Sex, gender, and aggression

If there is one thing about our subject of which most people feel completely sure, it is that aggression is a predominantly male characteristic. Warfare, violent crime, boxing, rough-and-tumble play: these and similar things are thought of overwhelmingly in our culture as male activities; all are seen as rooted in a basic tendency for males to be more aggressive than females. The power of this cultural presumption may be judged from the fact that although many laboratory studies do reveal sex differences in human aggression, those measuring behaviour 'objectively' generally find far smaller differences than do those measuring attitudes and beliefs by means of questionnaires in which people are asked to assess their own behaviour 'subjectively' (Frodi, Macaulay, and Thorne 1977). In other words, males and females tend to exaggerate such sex differences in aggression as there are, presumably because they believe that such differences ought to exist.

The fact that there are powerful norms and expectations about aggression and sex in our culture creates a major problem for the student of sex differences in human behaviour. The problem is simply this: in a rational, self-aware, and highly cultural species, the mere conviction that males are (or should be) more aggressive than females may itself serve to create and sustain these behavioural sex differences. In such a situation, adults may exemplify and teach a set of behavioural norms promoting greater amounts of aggression in boys than in girls; and when pressed, they may cite in support of their actions the 'naturalness' of a behaviour difference whose origin lies in their own and past generations of cultural belief and practice. As Richard Dawkins has pointed out (1982:12), when this occurs it is indeed true that male/female behaviour differences are 'genetically determined'; but they are so only because adults are using a genetic marker (male/female) as a basis for the differential treatment of children. Here is a case where culture may be directly creating a behaviour–genetic difference!

Before moving on, we must define the terms sex and gender. By sex differences, we shall mean distinctions between male and female that are based on particular biological criteria, such as the possession of particular chromosomes, organs, or other physical attributes; whereas by gender differences, we shall mean distinctions between male and female that are based on behavioural or social criteria, such as dress, bearing, or manner. The distinction is thus one of attribution, not one of substance, and as such, it does not beg the question of the relationship between genetic and social factors in the determination of maleness and femaleness. For many purposes, the distinction may be ignored; but not for all, as we shall see.

In an influential work, John Money and Anke Ehrhardt (1972) have analysed the complex developmental processes relating to sex and gender that follow on an initial genetic difference at conception. In the normal course of events, they suggest, these processes may be likened to a relay race: the 'baton' is passed from the genes (females generally possess two X chromosomes, males generally possess one X and one Y) to the gonads (females generally possess ovaries, males generally possess testes); from the gonads to the genitals (females generally possess a vagina, males generally possess a penis); from the genitals to those who attribute sex at birth; from the attributers to the subject of attribution in the formation of what Money and Ehrhardt call gender identity (the sense of being either male or female) in early childhood; and from gender identity to specific gender roles as individuals find their place within the wider culture.

Through their work with children whose sexual development has departed from this normal sequence in one way or another, Money and Ehrhardt have thrown much light on the interrelationships between these different stages. Take, for example, the case where genetic and gonadal sex are inconsistent with genital sex. Here, sex may be misattributed at birth; and if the mistake is not spotted fairly quickly, the young child may go on to acquire the wrong gender identity (wrong, that is, in terms of its genetic and gonadal constitution, and perhaps also in terms of the changes that may subsequently take place in its body at puberty). In such a case, parents and doctors face a difficult decision once the mistake has been spotted; for now, attributed sex is different from gender identity. The question thus arises, should the child's gender identity be changed so as to correspond to its newly discovered sex; or should the newly discovered sex be changed so as to correspond to its gender identity?

In many cases, Money and Ehrhardt believe that the latter alternative is preferable; and this, not because of the comparative ease of the relevant surgical and pharmacological procedures, but rather because of the sheer power of gender identity in a person's life and the very great psychological and social disruption that they believe may be involved in trying to change it. However, lest we should regard this as an inevitable fact about the human condition, it is worth noting that we know of cases where children appear to experience little or no difficulty in changing gender identities. For example, in the Dominican Republic there are children who have a rare metabolic disorder that delays the development of male characteristics until puberty. With the support of their culture, these children appear to make a smooth and untroubled transition from childhood femaleness to adolescent maleness (McGinnley 1979).

Kohlberg (1966, 1969) has written about the ways in which children analyse their social worlds. In forming gender concepts, they are more often influenced by cultural stereotypes than by the models provided by their own parents. As soon as the child has identified itself as male or female, Kohlberg suggests, it actively seeks out appropriate models and appropriate activities, taking charge, as it were, of its own socialization. Any parent who has tried to counteract the impact of wider society upon his or her own children knows the extent to which this is true, and it gives us at least a dim sense of what must be involved in a child's coming to terms with being a boy instead of a girl (or vice versa) in a situation where the wider society confers no obvious legitimacy upon a change. An entire personal and social world may be undermined by such a dilemma; and the extent of the damage gives us some idea of the power of culture in the shaping of gender differences.

For present purposes, the prime importance of Money and Ehrhardt's work is that it calls attention to the complexity of an apparently straightforward dichotomy that most of us simply take for granted in everyday life. It turns out that many naturally occurring human life histories blur the male/female distinction; and with appropriate surgical, pharmacological, and psychological assistance even more perfectly liveable variations are possible. In fact, Money and Ehrhardt's detailed interpretation of the 'relay race' of sex and gender determination has been extensively criticized by other workers. Indeed, to some extent their own descriptions of sex and gender development, and the diagram that accompanies them, belie their chosen metaphor: there are far too many branching and converging lines for the process to be very race-like; and, of course, influences between different levels in the specification of sex and gender are reciprocal – concentrations of sex hormone may set the physiological 'tone' for particular psychological and social experiences, for example, but, equally, psychological and social experiences may modify or reset the sex-hormone levels.

The subtlety of the interactions occurring during gender development makes the drawing of firm conclusions about causes from even the simplest of data on effects somewhat hazardous. For example, Money and Ehrhardt found that genetically female children who had experienced high levels of male sex hormone prenatally tended to be more 'tomboyish' and less interested in personal adornment than normal girls; and they suggested that the prenatal male sex hormones might have produced this effect by 'masculinizing' the nervous system (Money and Ehrhardt 1972). However, as they pointed out, it is also perfectly possible that postnatal processes may have been partly or totally responsible for the effect. One would like to know a great deal more, for example, about how these girls felt about their somewhat masculinized bodies and their considerably fraught medical histories (which often included genital surgery, hormone therapy, delayed onset of menstruation, and reproductive complications); for, of course, any or all of these factors may have been involved in the girls' de-emphasis of 'girlish' pursuits. We note this, not to undermine the possibility that hormones are involved in male/female behaviour differences in our culture, but simply to illustrate the complexity of the interactions that may be involved in the determination of even the most apparently clear-cut behavioural effects.

Thus, gender is a far from straightforward variable to be added into the developmental equation for aggressive behaviour. We have seen that there are different plausible explanations for the fact that, in our own culture, masculinity is associated with aggressivity. Perhaps sex-hormone levels in the embryo predispose boys growing up in our culture towards more 'boyish' pursuits, including more aggressive interactions with their peers; perhaps sex and gender attribution and differential treatment from birth onwards lead to the same thing; perhaps both of these factors play their part. One thing, however, is certain: sex, gender, and aggression do not map neatly and uniformly upon one another in development. Not only is there a wide range of individual variation in male and female behaviour within our own culture, but also there is a wide range of variation between cultures.

Looking to other cultures can help us form a better judgement of the relationship between sex, gender, and aggression. Many Javanese, for example, appear to operate with a notion of gender somewhat different from ours. Javanese women control the household finances, and they bargain tenaciously in the markets. The men are embarrassed by this bargaining, and they admit to being less able to handle money in a practical way. According to the Javanese, it is women's greater refinement that enables them to be more assertive; and this refinement is also reflected in their dominance of certain traditional arts such as dance and the making of batik cloth. Women do not participate in dances of strength and violence, which are considered masculine; and when men dance a more refined dance, this is considered higher art than when women do so, since the men had to suppress more in order to do so (A. Widodo, personal communication; and S. Brenner, unpublished manuscript). On the basis of these admittedly overgeneralized stereotypes, it appears that in Java both refinement and assertiveness are feminine attributes, whereas strength and violence are masculine. If we look for conflict in everyday life, it is Javanese women who appear to stand out; but if we look for conflict in far rarer and more extraordinary bouts of overt violence, then it is Javanese men who come to the fore. In this situation, then, which is the more aggressive sex?

Bending twig or emerging butterfly?

We began this chapter with an old saying about bending twigs. The most basic assumption underlying this saying is that there is continuity between early experience and adult life. In at least some minimal sense, of course, this must be true: without a very basic sort of psychological continuity, it would not be meaningful to speak of a single person as existing through long periods of time at all. At the same time, however, it is also true that time brings change. Children who set out with 'a good start in life' may later 'go wrong', and those who are less lucky to begin with may benefit from happier experiences later on.

Instead of the metaphor of the bent twig, perhaps we would be better off with the image of the emerging butterfly. From caterpillar through chrysalis to butterfly is not so much a quantitative step as a quantum leap. If a caterpillar were to be kept experimentally under conditions of complete darkness, we should hardly expect the butterfly that emerged in due course to react to light in a way completely different from that of normal butterflies. It might, of course; but the characteristics, capabilities, and needs of the two stages in the animal's life cycle are so utterly different that it seems highly unlikely.

People, of course, do not undergo a physical metamorphosis anything like that of many insects; but cognitive change through development is profound. While changes in physical size, at least, are more-or-less continuous throughout the period of growth, at a mental level it is more true to say that infants emerge from successive cognitive chrysalises as (hopefully) well-integrated social selves. These selves are thoughtful and they are conscious; they are conscious of themselves, and they are conscious of how they may or may not appear in the minds of others. To such beings, without parallel (so far as we know) in the rest of the animal world, the notions of personal efficacy and of self-esteem, and the emotions of honour, pity, pride, and shame are at least as important in the daily business of social interaction as are the zoologically more familiar notions of dominance and subordination, or the earthier emotions of anger, fear, and sexual desire.

Why, in the face of the metamorphic transformation of the more-or-less thoughtless and unselfconscious newborn infant into a mature human being, should we ever have expected any but the most superficial of continuities between babyish yelling and football terrace chanting; between preschool rough-and-tumble play and adolescent gang violence; between infantile 'undirected rage' and adult fury? The development of human aggression is intimately interwoven with new cognitions and motivations that make infancy as different from maturity as the life of a caterpillar is from that of a butterfly.

CHAPTER SEVEN

Models and mechanisms of aggression

The problem of motivation

Anyone who has kept or handled animals for any length of time knows that, just like people, they have their different moods. This is a colloquial way of saying that the same animal does not always react to the same stimuli in the same way. For one thing, there are often long-term, more-or-less irreversible changes associated with development. Male songbirds, for example, may start to sing in response to females or other males only when they are sexually mature. But in addition, animals are also subject to short-term, more-or-less reversible changes in responsiveness to a given stimulus. Thus, male songbirds may be more inclined to sing to females at some times of the year, or at some times of the day, than they are at others.

Such transient changes are of great significance in the study of animal behaviour. Quite apart from anything else, they suggest that a pure stimulus–response model of the causation of behaviour is likely to be inadequate. The fact that the same stimulus does not always evoke the same response from the same animal obliges us to consider the role of internal as well as external causal factors in the genesis of behaviour; it obliges us, in short, to consider the problem of motivation.

In humans, motivation is most easily studied by asking people why they are behaving in a particular way. However, this direct approach is obviously not possible with other animals; and instead, two quite distinct alternatives are commonly adopted. First, animals are studied behaviourally. Here, the object is to observe behaviour in a variety of different stimulus environments with a view to making inferences about the kinds of motivational mechanisms that are in place between stimulus 'inputs' and response 'outputs' somewhere within animals' nervous systems. Secondly, animals are studied physiologically. Here, the object is to establish by direct observation and experiment the nature of the motivational mechanisms themselves.

These two approaches may be compared with the two very different ways in which a car may be explored by a complete novice. The scientist who adopts a purely behavioural approach to the study of motivation is rather like a novice who learns about a car by playing with the driver's controls until he has learnt its response characteristics and mastered the art of driving; whereas the scientist who adopts a physiological approach is rather like a novice who learns about a car by getting underneath it until he has figured out exactly how it works. Obviously, both approaches have their place; and in the end, the task must be to combine them in a general theory of motivation.

Which ever approach to the study of motivation may be favoured, it is unlikely that much progress will be made without the construction of motivational models. Such models are schematic representations of the presumed characteristics of a motivational system, and their purpose is threefold: to summarize what is known of the system to date; to permit the prediction of new features of the system which may be open to further testing; and to enhance the degree of control that the experimenter has over the system by means of behavioural or physiological intervention.

There are two different kinds of motivational models – realistic and formal. A realistic model purports to represent the actual neurophysiological mechanisms underlying behaviour, whereas a formal model is concerned only to represent abstractly some important property or properties of these mechanisms. Realistic models are, of course, the ultimate goal of motivational analysis. However, the technical problems involved in their construction are considerable; and in most cases, we are obliged to make do with rather more formal schemata. Unfortunately, the distinction between realistic and formal models is by no means clear-cut. This is because in practice virtually all scientific models have analogical or metaphorical components, whereas even the most obviously formal representations usually attempt to incorporate at least some realistic assumptions. As a result, it can sometimes be quite difficult to determine what, if any, are the intended real-world implications of any particular behavioural model.

There are risks associated with behavioural modelling. For example, there is a risk that we may beguile ourselves with words, and simply assume that there must be a single mechanism responsible for all of the varied behaviour patterns that we have grouped together for our own analytic purposes under the descriptive heading 'aggression'. Again, having constructed a successful realistic model, we may come to presume that its physical representation must be a discrete neurophysiological structure or 'brain centre'. In reality, of course, there is no guarantee that the brain conforms to the dictates of our behavioural classifications; and if it should happen that we have modelled functions whose neurophysiological correlates are scattered throughout a number of different regions of the brain, then we may find ourselves chasing a structural will-o'-the-wisp.

This sort of thing has happened before in other branches of biology. For example, in an apt essay on 'The meaninglessness of protoplasm', Garrett Hardin (1956) noted that metabolic processes have often been compared to the combustion of fuel in an engine. This comparison invites the question, 'What is the biological "engine" that metabolizes?'; and to this question there may come back the answer, 'Why, the protoplasm, of course!'. But 'protoplasm' is merely a convenient fiction that serves to obscure rather than to clarify the fact that metabolism is a process rather than the operation of a physically defined structure. Hardin likens the phrase 'protoplasm metabolizes' to the phrase 'it is thundering'. What is the 'it' that thunders? – merely a grammatical invention! Our task must be to see that we do not substitute such grammatical inventions for genuine mechanisms in our attempts to model aggressive behaviour.

Knowledge, prediction, and control: these are the closely interrelated objects of motivational analysis. In this chapter, we shall be concerned with the attempt to know, predict, and control aggressive behaviour through the construction of models of what is presumed to be going on within the nervous systems of animals and humans when they threaten or attempt to inflict injury upon one another. We begin by considering one of the best-known and most influential of all the formal models of motivation to have come out of ethology. Significantly, this model has now been more-or-less completely discarded by ethologists, and a consideration of why this has happened will pave the way for the remainder of our discussion.

A bucketful of aggression?

Immediately after the Second World War, Konrad Lorenz (1950) set out an ingenious and rather striking model of the causation of all so-called 'instinctive' behaviour (for ease of reading we shall drop the use of 'scare marks' around the term instinct henceforth, but they should be taken as read). In retrospect, it is clear that this so-called 'psychohydraulic' model underlies not only the bulk of Lorenz's own theorizing about animal and human behaviour, both before and after 1950, but also the greater part of ethologists' theoretical work on instinct in the post-war period. Described colloquially and rather irreverently as the 'flush-toilet' model, Lorenz's influential contribution is still the most appropriate starting point for a consideration of the motivation of aggression.

The psychohydraulic model is best presented in diagrammatic form

(Figure 7.1). We are to assume that an animal has within its central nervous system as many distinct motivational 'energies' as it has specific instincts. Each distinct energy is likened to a body of water accumulating

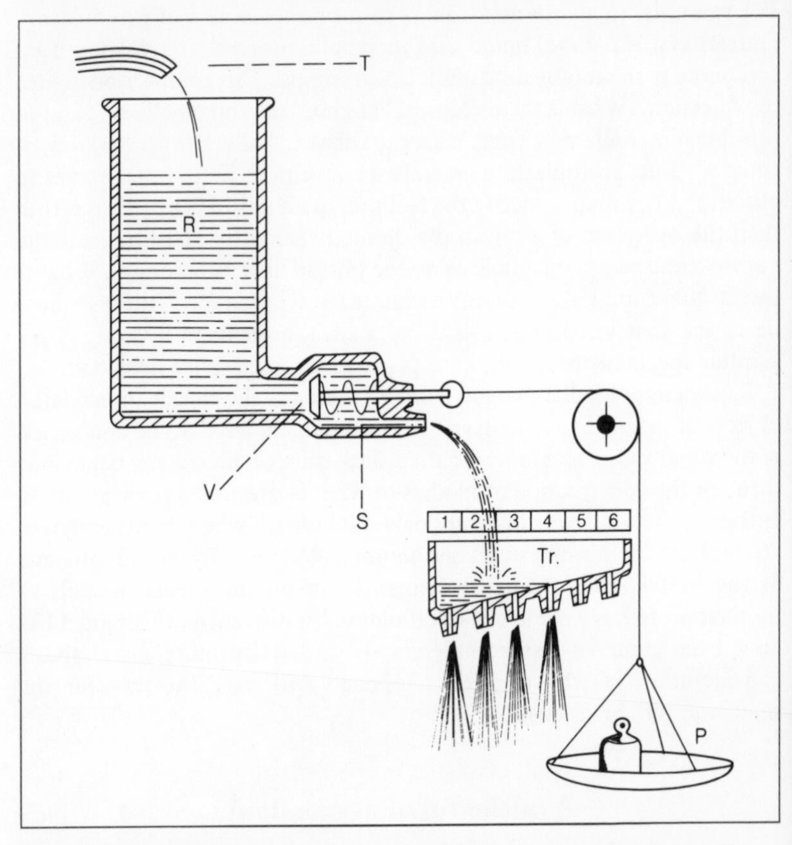

Figure 7.1 Konrad Lorenz's famous 'psychohydraulic' model of motivation. For an explanation of the features of so-called 'instinctive' behaviour that this model is intended to explain, see the discussion in the text. (After Lorenz 1950.)

continually in a reservoir so long as the relevant instinct is not being expressed. The water is prevented from escaping by a spring-loaded valve, and this may be opened, either by an appropriate water pressure or by an appropriate weight in a scale pan attached to the valve, or by some combination of the two. The water pressure represents a hypothetical impetus or 'drive' to the performance of an instinctive act, its release represents the performance itself, and the trough represents various behavioural movements or actions that together comprise the instinct. The weight in the scale pan represents one or more hypothetical 'releasing stimuli' that may be present in the animal's environment, and the valve represents a hypothetical 'innate releasing mechanism' connecting internal drive with external stimuli.

There is no doubt, of course, that Lorenz intended his psychohydraulic model to apply to conflict behaviour. In *On Aggression* (1966), for example, he portrayed aggression as an endogenous, instinctive energy that increases steadily with time and must sooner or later be released. Possessed of such energy in the context of modern, technological cultures, humans were uniquely dangerous; and their only hope of living less violently in the future lay in the diversion of instinctive aggression into comparatively harmless channels, such as competitive sport.

Without question, Lorenz's model was an important contribution to ethology. This is largely because it possessed all the hallmarks of a useful scientific model: it was (at least superficially) plausible; it was exceedingly simple; and above all, it had great predictive power. For if animals possess motivational mechanisms of the kind Lorenz proposed, then it should be possible to discover a series of quite separate unitary instincts possessed of the following characteristics:

1. Each instinct should be subject to the same general rules concerning the relationships between internal energy and external stimuli.
2. For each instinct there should be one or more specific and stereotyped behavioural actions released in response to one or more specific releasing stimuli.
3. The probability that any given instinctive act will occur should increase with time since its last performance.
4. With increasing time since its last performance, each instinctive act should be expressed even where appropriate releasing stimuli are very weak or even absent.
5. Each instinctive act should be capable of being temporarily 'exhausted' by repeated performance.
6. There should be no feedback from the early stages of instinctive action in the form of adjustment or cessation of later stages.

Such predictions as these inspired a large amount of ethological research in the 1950s and 1960s; and to begin with, the psychohydraulic model appeared to work quite well. Examples were found of behaviour patterns that appeared to be relatively stereotyped (the so-called fixed-action patterns); of behaviour patterns that appeared to be elicited by specific releasers (the so-called sign stimuli); of behaviour patterns the probability of whose performance appeared to increase with time since the last performance (e.g., some forms of sexual behaviour); and so on. Gradually, however, difficulties began to emerge. By reviewing the six major predictions of the model listed above, we shall see that although some of them appear to born out by some cases, all of them are falsified by numerous others.

First, what of the prediction that each instinct should be subject to the same general rules concerning the relationship between internal energy and external stimuli? Unfortunately, there is no evidence that any one animal possesses motivational mechanisms of the same general kind for different classes of its supposedly instinctive activity. For example, in one experiment with Siamese fighting fish, Hogan, Kleist, and Hutchings (1970) showed that, although the animals could be made to work increasingly hard for opportunities to eat, they could not be made to do so for opportunities to fight. The obvious reason for this disparity is that eating fulfils a regulatory or homeostatic function, whereas fighting does not; and the clear implication of this finding is that two quite different motivational mechanisms are involved. The first prediction is falsified.

Secondly, what of the prediction that for each instinct there should be one or more specific behavioural actions released by one or more specific stimuli? Here, there are a lot of cases that appear at first sight to fit the prediction quite well. Many fish and birds, for example, have been reported to respond to a limited range of specific 'sign stimuli' with an equally limited range of 'fixed-action patterns'. Yet even here things are not quite as the model predicts. Computer analysis of slow-motion film reveals that many so-called fixed-action patterns are in fact enormously variable, with behavioural components being varied and re-ordered both during a single performance and from one performance to the next (Klopfer 1974). Such variation probably reflects fine-scale tuning of behaviour in response to a changing environment, and this is something that the psychohydraulic model simply does not allow for at all.

Thirdly, what of the prediction that the probability with which any given instinct is performed should increase with time since its last performance? Certainly, some animals (such as laboratory mice) do show a progressive increase in aggressive behaviour when reintroduced to other members of their own species after progressively long periods of social isolation; but others (such as the cichlid fish *Haplochromis burtoni*) show exactly the opposite effect (Heiligenberg and Kramer 1972). In the case of the mice, it may be that regular social contact leads to the habituation of aggression; whereas in the case of the fish, it appears that social contact leads to the gradual accumulation of a hormone that makes fighting more likely. Here, then, we are faced not with a unitary psychohydraulic mechanism but rather with a likely diversity of motivational mechanisms affecting aggression in two different species.

Can instinctive behaviour be 'released' as a result of a sheer 'head' of motivational 'pressure' and in the absence of any appropriate eliciting stimulus? Lorenz provided one or two anecdotal examples of so-called vacuum activities; but such activities have not been widely reported in the literature. Indeed, we do not know of a single well-authenticated example of unelicited or 'vacuum' aggression in animals living in a relatively normal environment. (Obviously, animals subjected to severe stimulus or social deprivation may show a variety of more-or-less disturbed behaviour, including on occasions apparently unelicited self-injury; but the significance of such behavioural pathology for our understanding of undisturbed motivational processes is far from clear.)

What, then, about the opposite extreme from vacuum activity, namely so-called exhaustion? Some observations on, for example, sexual behaviour do seem at first sight to confirm the notion of exhaustion; but, once again, things are not quite what they seem. When placed with a receptive female, a male rat that has not mated for some time will perform a series of mounts culminating in an ejaculation, then rest, then perform another series of mounts and an ejaculation, then rest again, and so on. The length of each rest increases with time until finally sexual behaviour ceases altogether.

This certainly looks like exhaustion! Yet in the early stages of this process, the number of mounts required to achieve an ejaculation actually decreases with time, which implies that the rat is becoming increasingly sensitized to (or more excited by) the female; and even after sexual behaviour has ceased altogether, the introduction of another receptive female initiates further mounting and ejaculation. So what, exactly, is being 'exhausted' here? Even in the case of sexual behaviour, where the evidence is at first sight most supportive of the idea of exhaustion, closer examination reveals that the psychohydraulic model is once again inadequate.

Finally, we come to the prediction that there should be no feedback from the consequences of instinctive actions in the form of behaviour adjustment or cessation. On reflection, this is really the most extraordinary limitation for an ethologist to impose upon a model of behaviour motivation. For it clearly makes no functional sense whatever for animals in their natural environments to be committed to all-or-nothing actions that are incapable of adjustment in response to their immediate consequences; and in fact, very few animals are ever so committed. On the contrary, feedback influences on behaviour are commonplace; and a growing recognition of their importance in behaviour has played a prominent part in the decline of the psychohydraulic model in recent years.

One example under this heading must suffice. In the rut, red deer stags engage in escalated fights involving roaring contests, parallel walking, and head clashes; but how far any given fight goes, who initiates the first direct attack, and who eventually gives way, are all dictated by what one contestant does in response to the moves that are being made by the other (Clutton-Brock and Albon 1979). Just imagine the fate of some poor psychohydraulic stag who, upon entering such a contest in his first season as a mature animal, was unfortunate enough to be burdened with a bucketful of aggression (i.e., a full Lorenzian aggression reservoir). Responding massively to the slightest provocation from older and stronger animals all around him, such a stag would almost certainly suffer severe injury in his very first contest; and his chances of living to fight another day, let alone of ever having any offspring, would be slim indeed. This, presumably, is one very good reason why Lorenzian aggression reservoirs have never evolved.

No motivational model that fails on so many separate predictive counts can possibly be adequate even in principle to the explanation of the causation of aggressive behaviour. Clearly, therefore, the psychohydraulic model has to go; and with it, and for essentially the same reasons, must go all other energy models of the motivation of aggressive behaviour. Included under this heading are not only the early theories of William McDougall (1908) but also those of Sigmund Freud (Strachey 1966–74). If action-specific energies will not suffice to explain the evidence, nor yet will irrational goal-directed tendencies, or mystical death wishes bubbling up from the unconscious mind to find expression in everything from self-hatred to international warfare.

Freud's ideas were expressed in metaphor and myth rather than in the operational terms of science, and it is at once pointless and presumptuous to dissect them in the context of current thinking about motivation. As Catherine Bateson (1972) has remarked, the metaphors of poetry allow for the expression of insights precluded by the literalities of prose, which is why perhaps even science needs its poets. Leaving aside, however, whatever poetic merits Freud's writings on aggression may have, it is arguable that their chief importance lies in their sanctioning before a wide public of the notion of the beast within. As we have already seen, there are many sound reasons for laying to rest the idea of the beast within. One more sound reason is that we have searched for the wellspring of the beast's amazing power, and we have failed to find it.

The search for a better model

To be fully adequate to the explanation of aggression, our models must be consistent with the highest possible degree of complexity, diversity, flexibility, and subtlety at the behavioural level. As we have seen, Lorenz's psychohydraulic model has been shown to fail on most or all of these counts. In recent years, therefore, the hunt has been on for a more satisfactory substitute. At the present time, there is no obvious and generally agreed candidate for this important role. Instead, ethologists and psychologists are currently pursuing a variety of different approaches (for reviews, see Toates 1980, 1983; Mcfarland 1985).

One of the more promising classes of motivational model currently under consideration is based upon the extremely simple idea of a 'negative feedback' system that works in much the same way as a thermostat. A thermostat works by continually comparing the actual temperature with some ideal temperature, which is represented by a predetermined 'set point'. By switching on a heating system whenever the temperature falls significantly below, and switching it off whenever the temperature rises significantly above this set point, the thermostat regulates the temperature (Figure 7.2).

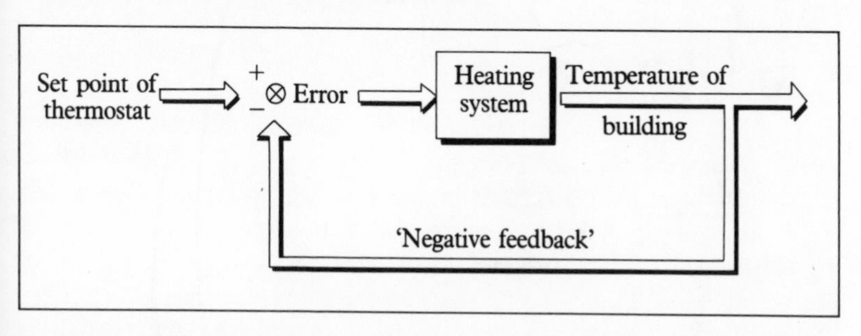

Figure 7.2 A domestic thermostat is a simple 'negative feedback' device that compares the actual temperature of a building with a predetermined set point. If the building temperature is too high, the heating system is switched off; if the building temperature is too low, the heating system is switched on. In this way, the system works to maintain the building temperature at the set point.

We may imagine an elementary motivational system working along much the same lines. Like a thermostat, such a system incorporates a preferred state in the form of a neurophysiological set point. Sensory inputs to the system are continuously monitored; and the motivational system initiates appropriate corrective action whenever these inputs indicate a significant departure from the set point.

A psychophysiological model of arousal and emotion incorporating these basic elements was proposed by Karl Pribram and Frederick T. Melges in 1969 (Pribram and Melges 1969; see also Miller, Galanter, and Pribram 1960). At the heart of this model is a so-called TOTE (test-operate-test-exit) system that works to achieve congruence between an internal set point, which may be taken to represent the system's 'expectation', and any actual sensory input, which may be taken to represent 'reality' (Figure 7.3). So long as there is a match between expectation and reality, the system maintains the status quo; but any mismatch produces an immediate alert ('arousal') followed by a process of appraisal.

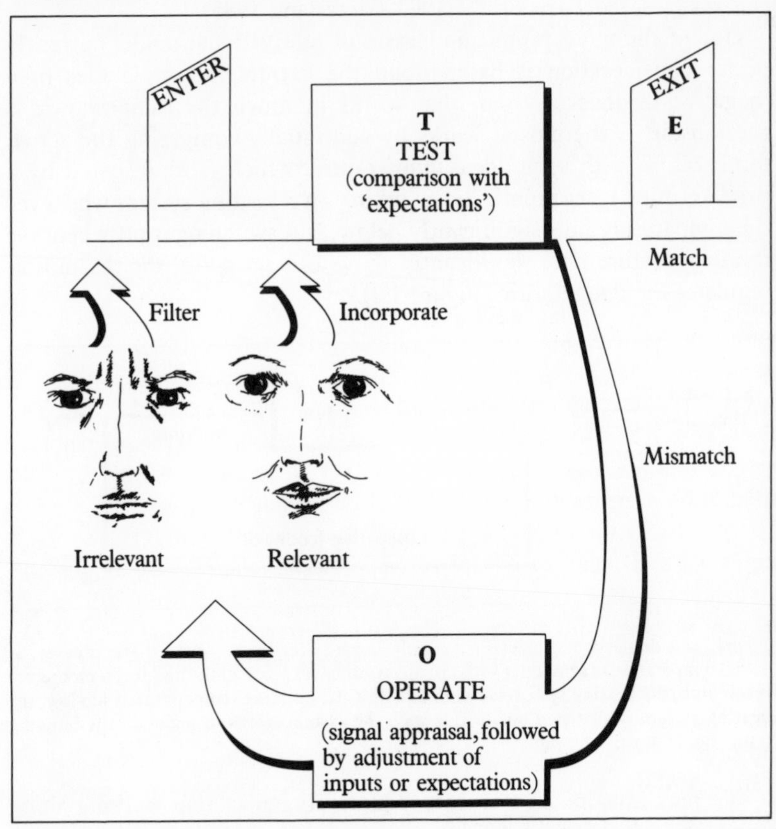

Figure 7.3 In this model, sensory inputs 'enter' the system and are 'tested' to determine whether they match expectations. If they do, they 'exit' immediately. If they do not, they are 'operated' upon until such time as a match is achieved. Following appraisal, 'irrelevant' inputs are filtered, while 'relevant' ones are incorporated into the test-template in the form of a modified expectation. Rather like the domestic thermostat (Figure 7.2), this system works to maintain congruence between sensory inputs and set points. (Original illustration by J. Parrish.)

At this point, the TOTE model becomes considerably more sophisticated than a thermostat. For the process of appraisal is presumed to allow for the possibility of modifying the original set point. If any given mismatched input is judged 'irrelevant' then, like a thermostat, the TOTE system initiates change until such time as the expected input is achieved; but if the mismatched input is judged 'relevant', it may be incorporated into the set point, with the result that congruence is restored at some new preferred state. The changes that are initiated by the system to restore congruence may include both the blocking of sensory inputs and the alteration of behaviour so as to change these inputs in the preferred direction.

There are several points worth noting about the TOTE model. First, the model is formal, providing no direct link with brain structures. Secondly, the model is psychophysiological, being applicable both to animals that do not have conscious awareness (in which case 'appraisal' and 'judgement' are metaphorical terms applying to purely physical processes), and to those that do (in which case appraisal and judgement may or may not be literal terms applying to what is going on in an animal's consciousness). Thirdly, the model incorporates previous experience within the system. Set points are not necessarily fixed for all time, but may be modified in the light of changing circumstances. Obviously, this raises important questions about how set points are established in the first place, as well as about the rules for their modification; but the main point here is that, at least in principle, the TOTE model provides for the integration of many different factors in behaviour motivation.

It is not difficult to get at least an intuitive grasp of how a TOTE system might work. During a dash to the airport, a parade may be judged an irrelevant nuisance; whereas during a relaxed Sunday afternoon drive, it may be just the thing to stay and watch. The appraisal that goes on in situations such as these appears to be related to the possession of both internal representations of the world or 'cognitive maps' (in this case, what the airport is, how to get there, what to expect along the way, etc.) and preferred states or 'purposes' (in this case, getting to the airport).

In addition, such appraisal appears to be related to emotional experience. The sight of a parade blocking the street during a dash to the airport may cause us to feel anxious, frustrated, or even angry; whereas the sight of the same thing on a Sunday afternoon drive may generate a variety of far more pleasant feelings. Karl Pribram argued that the emotions are of two general types: 'retrospective' emotions, which represent conscious awareness of incongruity within a TOTE system; and 'prospective' emotions, which represent conscious awareness of the mechanisms that seek to overcome such incongruity in one or other of the ways outlined above.

The TOTE model can be applied to aggressive behaviour. It is conceivable that feelings of anger or hostility are perceptions of incongruity between set points and actual sensory inputs to a hypothetical TOTE system; and similarly, it is conceivable that a great deal of aggressive behaviour represents the corrective output of such a system attempting to restore a preferred sensory input. On this view, the flexibility of so much aggressive behaviour may reflect the sheer sophistication with which TOTE systems direct their output so as to achieve their set points; and the openness of so much aggression to change through learning may reflect the degree to which set points are modified by experience. Finally, the cognitive and emotional dimensions to the TOTE system, at least in humans, may provide a bridge between brain mechanisms and the kinds of thoughts and feelings about aggression that have been discussed in earlier chapters of the book.

The TOTE system has been incorporated by the psychologist W.T. Powers (1973) into a more general and a more realistic model of motivation. For Powers, the purpose of any particular behaviour is to prevent a perception from changing. An animal has a 'reference condition', or controlled perception, which may be either developmentally fixed or developmentally flexible. Unless and until this reference condition is altered, however, the animal's behaviour can have only two classes of effects: it may alter the state of the world, and thus modify the sensory input at source; or it may alter the state of the animal's physiology, and thus modify the sensory input somewhere between the animal's sense organs and its motivational mechanisms. Either class of effect, of course, alters the perception that is to be compared to the reference condition.

Powers conceives of the behaving animal's nervous system as hierarchically organized, with higher-level systems controlling lower. Only the lowest-level systems interact directly with the environment, which is perceived initially in terms of intensity signals. Second-level systems bring sensation, while higher-order systems deal with information concerning the configuration and sequence of inputs, the relationships between different classes of inputs, the setting of priorities of outputs, and so forth. For Powers, the entire hierarchy is to be regarded as serving to control perceptions. If a controlled perception is threatened by inappropriate sensory inputs, then behaviour is reorganized until the error signal disappears.

It is a major implication of this sort of motivational model that it requires a totally different method of classifying behaviour from that which we have seen in older instinct theories. This point is well illustrated in a simple example provided by the Dutch neurophysiologist Alexander Cools (1985). One rat is bitten by another. What happens next? Adopting the perspective that we have been describing, we may say that the bitten rat's preferred state or reference condition is to avoid being bitten again. Accordingly, it selects one or more among a very wide range of behaviour patterns, varying from lateral threat to freezing. This selection depends upon both the bitten rat's previous experience and its immediate circumstances; and it is governed by the functional criterion of the successfulness of any particular behavioural option in moving the rat towards its reference condition. In terms of conventional behaviour classification, lateral threat and freezing belong to the distinct classes of offensive and defensive behaviour, respectively. In terms of the Powers/Cools model, however, both belong to the same class; for both forms of behaviour control sensory input with respect to a single reference condition.

The great virtue of this way of viewing behaviour is that potentially it can make coherent and sensible connections between putative brain mechanisms and the functional analysis of behaviour. For instead of searching for the discrete neurophysiological representations of arbitrary behaviour patterns (e.g., 'biting an opponent') or arbitrary instincts (e.g., 'aggression'), the Powers/Cools approach invites us to search for those functionally meaningful goals, set points, or reference conditions that are embedded within complex and flexible hierarchies of negative feedback control.

In support of this strategy, Cools (1985) notes three important features of the cerebral organization of behaviour: (1) the existence of a high degree of freedom in the programming of specific behavioural states; (2) the absence of cerebral representation of specific behavioural states at any but the lowest levels in the hierarchy; and (3) the rapid and flexible recruitment of successively higher-level functions in 'frustrating' situations (i.e., situations in which an animal is unable to correct a mismatch by behavioural activity at a particular level in the hierarchy).

If there is any merit in this approach to the study of motivation, then we are unlikely to find the single term aggression of very much help to us in our attempts to model the neurophysiological mechanisms subserving conflict behaviour. This is because, as we have stressed repeatedly throughout this book, the term aggression groups together a great variety of behaviour patterns that serve a great variety of functions in the day-to-day lives of animals and people; and, according to the Powers/Cools model, therefore, we should expect to find many different neural elements involved in their control. For much the same reason, of course, the Powers/Cools model makes it unlikely that the neurophysiological representation of all aggressive behaviour is confined to a single part of the brain. It is to this controversial topic that we turn next.

Aggression: a localizable problem?

Phrenology, old and new

For almost two centuries, there has been a close link between theories of 'innate mental faculties' or instincts and the idea of localization of functions within the central nervous system. Localization theory is important in the present context for at least two reasons: first, at a theoretical level it has (literally) embodied enduring assumptions about the unitary nature of aggression; and, secondly, at a practical level it has underpinned a considerable amount of clinical intervention designed to reduce or abolish altogether one or another kind of undesirable aggressive impulse. In this field, more than most, what people have thought about the nature of aggression has influenced what they have thought it appropriate to do about aggressive behaviour in the domain of everyday human affairs.

All modern localization theory has its origins in the work of the early nineteenth-century phrenologists. According to the phrenologists, the mind was composed of a large number of discrete mental faculties, ranging from rather earthy things (such as 'combativeness' and 'philoprogenitiveness') to rather aetherial things (such as 'veneration' and 'the spirit of metaphysics'). Supposedly, these mental faculties were distributed across the surface of the brain according to a number of simple laws, such that the psychological characteristics of individuals, races, and species were reflected in readily measurable cranial and facial differences.

Although in its heyday it was a fashionable and a widely accepted science, phrenology fell rapidly into disrepute in the late Victorian period. In particular, its craniometric technique quickly degenerated from the level of high science to that of parlour game or even vaudeville. Nevertheless, phrenology left its mark on brain science in the form of an enduring tradition of research on the cerebral localization of mental functions (Young 1970). In the late nineteenth century, first language, and then a variety of sensorimotor functions came to be located in specific parts of the cerebrum. By the turn of the century, the most elaborate brain maps were once again available; and one commentator referred to them aptly as 'New Phrenology' (Franz 1912).

The beast within the brain

Central to a great deal of early localization work was a modified version of the idea of the beast within, according to which the brain is to be understood as a hierarchy of distinct structural and functional levels; a hierarchy in which each successive level, corresponding to a particular phase of evolutionary history, restrains and controls the one beneath it. This idea was prominent in the work of the mid-Victorian neurologist John Hughlings Jackson (who got it from the evolutionary philosopher Herbert Spencer), and it found its way into a great deal of neurology and neurophysiology in the first half of the twentieth century, up to and including the work of Paul MacLean, which was discussed more fully in Chapter 2.

Thus, for example, the Harvard physiologist Walter Cannon and his associates used the Jacksonian idea of a hierarchy of restraint to explain the elicitation of 'sham rage' in cats following surgical removal of the forebrain. By excising successively larger amounts of tissue, Cannon and his co-workers were able to show that an area of the midbrain known as the hypothalamus was essential to the production of sham rage (Cannon and Britton 1925; Bard 1934). Similarly, the Yale neurophysiologist John Fulton and his associates used the Jacksonian notions of hierarchy and restraint to account for behavioural changes in primates following experimental damage to the frontal lobes (Fulton and Ingraham 1929; Fulton and Jacobsen 1935). In each case, the idea was that lower, more primitive brain centres for instinct and emotion were 'released' into spontaneous activity by the removal of higher, more advanced centres for intelligence and learning.

The work of Cannon and Fulton depended largely upon the technique of ablation – that is, they simply removed areas of their animals' brains under anaesthetic, and then observed the results on recovery. In the early 1930s, however, the German neurophysiologist Walter Hess (1932–8) advanced the study of the localization of aggression by using a stereotaxic device to stimulate small areas of the brains of unanaesthetized cats. In this way, he was able to elicit directly by positive intervention what Cannon and his associates had revealed by negative ablation. Stimulation of specific areas of the hypothalamus caused a cat to behave just as it would when confronted by a dog – its fur stood on end, it spat and growled, it extended its claws, and so on.

Using his new technique, Hess went on to map the cat's midbrain in some detail (Hess 1954). By demonstrating that it is possible to identify small, relatively discrete brain areas whose stimulation elicits relatively specific behaviour patterns, he encouraged the hope that from such work would come a clearer understanding of the neurophysiological mechanisms subserving a great deal of complex behaviour. Following Hess's lead, other workers went on to identify so-called centres not only for aspects of aggression but also for pain, pleasure, and sexual behaviour (see, for example, Heath, Monroe, and Micler 1955; Olds 1955; King 1961; Flynn, Venegas, and Edwards 1970). In 1949, Hess's contribution to brain science was recognized by the award of the Nobel Prize for Physiology and Medicine, which he shared with the Portuguese neurologist Egas Moniz.

Localization and psychosurgery

Walter Hess's Nobel Prize was certainly well-deserved; but the fact that he was honoured alongside Egas Moniz serves to remind us of both the theoretical weaknesses and the practical dangers of so much localization research. For Moniz was the man who first applied the preliminary results of early localization research on the functions of the brain's frontal lobes in the treatment of human subjects suffering from a variety of behavioural disturbances; and in doing so, he became the modern founder of that most ill-conceived of all psychiatric adventures – psychosurgery.

Moniz's move into psychosurgery came about in the following way. In 1935, he attended the Second International Neurological Congress in London, where he heard a short paper read by John Fulton. In this paper, Fulton gave the preliminary results of an experiment involving the removal of the frontal lobes of two adolescent female chimpanzees, named Becky and Lucy (Fulton and Jacobsen 1935). In addition to a specific and profound loss of intellectual function, he reported that frontal lobotomy appeared to have induced a more general emotional change in the direction of greater placidity. Becky, in particular, had been prone to violent temper tantrums, and in test situations she had easily developed so-called experimental neurosis. After lobotomy, however, these behavioural characteristics had disappeared completely. As Fulton's colleague Carlyle Jacobsen put it, 'It was as if the animal had joined the "happiness cult of the Elder Micheaux", and had placed its burdens on the Lord!' (Jacobsen, Wolfe and Jackson 1935).

According to Fulton (1949), after he had read his paper 'Dr Moniz arose and asked if frontal-lobe removal prevents the development of experimental neuroses in animals and eliminates frustrational behaviour, why would it not be possible to relieve anxiety states in man by surgical means?'. Within a matter of months, and with the help of his colleague Almeida Lima, Moniz had set about answering his own question by destroying parts of the frontal lobes of 20 patients. In Moniz's view (1936), the results of this treatment were extremely encouraging; and notwithstanding the fact that he was assaulted and seriously injured by one of his own patients (for whom the technique of surgical pacification had evidently been less than wholly successful), he was eventually awarded a Nobel Prize 'for the discovery of the therapeutic value of prefrontal leucotomy in certain psychoses'.

After 1935, localization research on animals and surgical attempts to control mentally disturbed people advanced hand in hand. Nowhere was the interdependence between the two areas more obvious than in Fulton's own laboratory at Yale, where after the Second World War there grew up an active programme of research in the overlapping fields of neurophysiology and psychosurgery. Fulton had two aims: first, to explain the mixture of desirable and undesirable effects that were being produced by the rapidly growing number of frontal lobotomies in the United States; and, secondly, to persuade psychosurgeons to refine these techniques with the help of new methods of brain manipulation and in the light of new data on frontal lobe function (Fulton 1951).

Among Fulton's colleagues at Yale in the early 1950s were the American neuroanatomist Paul MacLean, whose thoroughly Jacksonian conception of the 'limbic system' has been described in Chapter 2, and the Spanish neurophysiologist José Delgado. These men collaborated for a time in the exploration of the frontotemporal region of the limbic system using Delgado's newly invented 'stimoceiver' (MacLean and Delgado 1953). This device enabled the neurophysiologist simultaneously to record from and to stimulate chosen brain targets; the idea was to detect supposedly pathological activity in a particular brain region, and then to intervene electrically to control or eliminate it.

Over the years, Delgado invented a whole series of ever more sophisticated devices of this kind. In the early 1960s, he attracted considerable attention by making a film that portrayed him successfully controlling a charging bull by means of a remote-controlled device embedded in the animal's brain (Delgado 1964) (Figure 7.4); and in the late 1960s, he used a similar device in an attempt to control the aggressive outbursts of seriously disturbed human subjects (Delgado, Mark et al. 1968). By the late 1970s, he was taking advantage of microelectronics in order to construct computer-controlled implants so small that they could be embedded more-or-less invisibly beneath his patients' scalps (Delgado 1981).

Throughout all of Delgado's work on brain and behaviour there has run the theme of brain and mind control. In an extraordinary book entitled *Physical Control of the Mind: Toward a Psycho-Civilized Society* (1969), Delgado made the case for the elevation of physical techniques of brain manipulation to the level of a major force in the shaping of future society. The human race, he reminded his readers, was in urgent need of being rescued from itself, and particularly from a potentially lethal

Figure 7.4 José Delgado included this most dramatic illustration of the technique of electrical stimulation of the brain in his James Arthur Lecture 'Evolution of physical control of the brain' (Delgado 1965). His own caption reads: 'A bull in full charge may be suddenly stopped by radio stimulation of the anterior part of the thalamus'.

combination of 'innate' aggression and enormous technological power. Fortunately, the problem that technology had created – bombs and missiles – it would also cure, in the form of brain implants.

Basing his claims upon a theory of the 'fragmental representation of behaviour' in the brain, Delgado looked forward to the further elaboration of electronic devices to the point where they could act as 'a master control of human behaviour by means of man-made plans and instruments'. The object of civilization, he suggested, should be to permit brain science to 'create a future man with greater personal freedom and originality, a member of a psycho-civilized society, happier, less destructive, and better-balanced than present man'. The old temple inscription 'Know Thyself' should now be replaced by a new sign over the brain laboratory entrance, 'Construct Thyself'.

Escape from psychocivilization

In *Physical Control of the Mind*, Delgado acknowledges that 'The prospect of any degree of physical control of the mind provokes a variety of objections: theological ... moral ... ethical ... philosophical'. Well, indeed it does, and so it should. The idea of turning people into bionic robots is offensive to our most basic notions of the autonomy, the integrity, and the human value of human beings; and, of course, it raises nightmarish political considerations to do with who, in this Brave New 'psychocivilized' World, is supposed to engineer whom, and for what purposes. But leaving aside these considerations, it is interesting to note that Delgado's list does not include the possibility that there might also be straightforward scientific objections to the idea of physical control of the mind. Apparently, it has not occurred to Delgado that there are any logical or biological obstacles in the path of inserting electrodes into people's heads as a means to the better regulation of human affairs.

But, of course, there are. First, the data on which most claims for the localization of function are based are extremely weak. For much of its history, localization research has depended upon ablation; and here, the temptation has always been to assume that a function is localized when its permanent loss follows damage to some circumscribed brain area. The error of this view is immediately obvious from a consideration of how long a television repair operative would be likely to stay in business by working with the same assumption. Even when the technique of stimulation is used alongside ablation, things are not as simple or as straightforward as many researchers appear to believe. The techniques themselves are always artificial, and often imprecise; and their effects are usually very variable. Rarely are studies sufficiently well controlled to permit firm conclusions about the relationships between specific brain areas and specific behaviour patterns.

Thus, in a careful review of the extensive literature on brain stimulation and aggression in monkeys, apes, and humans, Plotnik (1974) concluded that virtually all the existing data were unreliable. Specifically criticizing the work of Delgado, along with that of many other workers, he commented rather bluntly that, in the case of the primates, 'If a writer insists that brain stimulation has shown that neural centers or triggers for aggression exist, this insistence is based on two subjects'. This hardly seems a firm empirical foundation for the construction of a 'psychocivilized' society.

If establishing a secure claim regarding the localization of a behavioural function is hard, interpreting its significance is often difficult to the point of impossibility. For the second great weakness of much localization research is that it seeks to substitute structure for function, and anatomy for psychophysiology. For simply knowing that any particular neuroanatomical locus is somehow or other involved in the genesis or abolition of a specific behaviour pattern is quite different from having an adequate psychophysiological theory concerning the nature of that behaviour, its organization, and its control; and it is such a theory that one needs in order to be able to assess both the likely effects of any particular surgical intervention and its likely significance in the future life of the subject. If you wish to modify or mend your telephone line, you had better understand how your telephone system works; merely knowing the address of your telephone company, or even the precise location of your telephone exchange, is not really very much use.

It is perhaps because of a tendency to substitute crude information on functional localization for adequate functional theories that Delgado operates with a totally misconceived contrast between psychological and environmental influences on behaviour, on the one hand, and brain mechanisms of behaviour, on the other. To read *Physical Control of the Mind* is to enter a weird universe in which people's experiences and thoughts somehow compete with their brains as potential causes of their behaviour. But, of course, this is quite absurd. It is the task of brain science to discover those neurophysiological mechanisms by which we experience and think about the world, not to set up such mechanisms as alternatives to these activities. Delgado's vision of the future is nightmarish not because he wants to turn people into robots but because he thinks of them as robots to start with.

We have taken Delgado's work as just one, albeit rather striking, example from the much larger field of psychosurgery. Of course, not all psychosurgeons have had either Delgado's taste for the theatrical or his obsession with the technocratic control of human behaviour; but the same trends are apparent throughout the field. The history of psychosurgery, for aggressive behavioural disturbances as for much else, is the history of the imposition of crude, quasi-phrenological maps upon the brain as the basis for the most dramatic and far-reaching of surgical interventions; in short, it is the history of ignorance masquerading as expert knowledge (Valenstein 1974, 1986; Chorover 1979).

If this appears a harsh judgement, consider the recent verdict of two other commentators on this field. In the course of a detailed study, the British psychologists Mark O'Callaghan and Douglas Carroll (1982) note two features of psychosurgery: first, its theoretical base has always been, and remains, pathetically weak – 'In summary', they write, 'we can only lament with previous reviewers that the rationales for psychosurgery lack both substance and consistency'; but, secondly, and what is even worse, after half a century of psychosurgical practice there is still no adequate evidence that it works. Such evidence as there is, O'Callaghan and Carroll argue, suggests that several standard operations – such as ablation of the amygdala, which has been widely performed in an attempt to cure so-called 'pathological aggression' – 'attract dismally low rates of substantial clinical improvement'. In no single case, in fact, do they find clinical evidence sufficient to justify continuing with the practice of psychosurgery.

In the 1980s, thankfully, the long-standing association between localization research and psychosurgery is beginning at last to dissolve. This is due in part to a growing (and long overdue) recognition of the limitations of localization studies alone to advance our understanding of brain function, and in part to the decline of psychosurgery as either a scientifically or a morally acceptable form of psychiatric treatment. Although there is no room for complacency, we may at least be permitted to hope that brain scientists will never again accept the easy equation of map-making with a mature theory of the brain mechanisms subserving human behaviour.

Conclusion

In this chapter, we have covered a number of different topics, from the problems of model construction to the inadequacies of psychosurgery. These topics are all closely interrelated, for each of them raises in a slightly different way the same basic question: how are we to understand the internal mechanisms subserving behaviour in general, and aggressive behaviour in particular? Clearly, we have not even attempted to give a complete answer to this question. Rather, our aims have been altogether more modest: first, we have tried to indicate how difficult is the task of constructing an adequate model of the motivational processes by which aggression is regulated; and secondly, by examining several influential lines of research, we have tried to suggest that a basic assumption contained within much previous work on models and mechanisms of aggression may be at the root of some of our present difficulties.

Much of the classical work on models and mechanisms of aggression assigned specific behavioural actions to specific instincts or specific brain centres. It assumed that the release of these instincts or the stimulation of these centres was the necessary and sufficient condition for the performance of specific aggressive acts. Our aim in contrasting the Lorenzian with the Powers/Cools model of behaviour motivation was to suggest that this classical approach rests on an elementary category mistake by which terms coined for one purpose at one level of analysis are carried over for quite different purposes at an altogether different level of analysis. Why should the brain correspond in its detailed structure and functioning to the abstract classifications that we have invented in order to help us get some sort of a handle on its vastly complex outputs?

Irrespective of its truth (and it should be noted that it has not been offered here as a definitive solution to the problem of motivation), the Powers/Cools model at least has the great virtue that it helps us to reconceive the brain mechanisms subserving behaviour in terms other than those of 'common-sense' behavioural classification. In addition, of course, it has the added advantage of discouraging us from the perennially popular idea that, by localizing aggression somewhere in the brain, we shall be able the better to manage it. The time has come to recognize that there simply is not some aggressive 'thing' inside our heads to be reasoned with, restrained, or removed.

Perhaps, as Catherine Bateson (1972) records, the role of particular neurones in the brain is rather like the role of particular letters in a sentence. The sentence 'Aggression is an unhelpful construct from the point of view of brain function' has a particular meaning in the context of this chapter; but it would be quite absurd to suppose that this meaning can be deciphered in the individual letters of which the sentence is composed. To understand the meaning of the individual letters themselves, it is not sufficient to understand the arguments of this chapter; we require in addition a knowledge of English grammar and syntax. It is for want of a proper understanding of the grammar and syntax of the brain that we currently find it so difficult to trace the relationships between nervous mechanisms and aggressive behaviour.

CHAPTER EIGHT

The evolution of animal and human conflict

Darwinism and behaviour

The Darwinian theory of evolution by natural selection is an essential ingredient in our understanding of aggressive behaviour. Without it, we would have no way of assessing the meaning or the significance of the conflicts and contests that go on between individual animals and groups of animals in nature. Moreover, without it we would have no way of assessing the a priori plausibility of any number of possible mechanisms of aggression that are based partly or wholly upon laboratory investigations. Why is there aggressive behaviour at all? What forms should we expect aggression to take? To what influences should we expect aggression to be subject? These and related questions are impossible to answer without considering the way in which behaviour may evolve by natural selection.

It is vital at the outset to have a clear grasp of the nature of Darwinian evolutionary analysis. To begin with, consider a hypothetical biological character. This may be anything at all, from the thickness of a bone to the degree of dispersal of offspring after achieving independence. To get started with our analysis, we must begin with alternate expressions of the character. In the first case, these might be 'thin bones' and 'thick bones'; and in the second, they might be 'all offspring stay at home', 'females stay at home, males disperse', 'all offspring disperse', and so on. Such alternate expressions of a character we shall term traits.

Traits need not be discrete – weight, height, etc. may be perfectly good ones, even though they vary continuously; they need not be deterministic – a perfectly good trait might be, for example, the learning of a particular association with a particular probability; they need not be permanent – a trait is just one possible characteristic of an organism, and along with all the rest, it may change with changing circumstances; and, finally, although in principle they may be caused by any combination of genetic and environmental factors, to be of any evolutionary consequence traits must be associated with genetic differences between individuals.

Having identified a trait, the Darwinian evolutionist attempts to resolve its consequences into 'costs' and ' benefits'. By costs and benefits we mean the penalties and rewards that a trait confers upon an organism's 'classical fitness'; and by classical fitness we mean an individual's expected lifetime reproductive success. All traits carry some fitness costs (after all, even the production of successful spermatozoa means that less energy and raw materials are available for other activities); but only some traits carry any fitness benefits, let alone enough benefits to make then evolutionarily successful. What matters for evolutionary purposes is the balance between costs and benefits for each available trait in a given population. Once this is known, we can say with some confidence that, other things being equal, natural selection will favour the trait that maximizes fitness.

At this point, the work of most Darwinian evolutionists is very nearly done. This is not to say, of course, that their work is particularly easy. On the contrary, identifying traits, determining their costs and benefits, combining these costs and benefits in ways that adequately reflect biological reality, and then deducing what will be the influence of natural selection in situations where other things may or may not always be equal – all these things can be very difficult; but where we are considering the evolution of ordinary characters – bones, wings, or navigational abilities, for example – trait analysis of this kind will normally suffice. The same is no longer true, however, when what we are interested in is social behaviour. For now, two vitally important complications must be taken into account.

Taking account of relatives

First, when analysing the evolution of social behaviour, our measure of classical fitness must be amended. The classical notion of fitness captures the essence of Darwin's theory, which is that what counts in evolution is the relative success with which particular genetic variants are propagated down the generations. This definition assumes (what is true for most purposes) that genes are propagated exclusively through the production of offspring. In reality, however, there is another important method of gene propagation, namely through the production of close genetic relatives; and this provides for an important variation in the process of natural selection – 'kin selection'.

Consider a gene that causes an individual to forego having its own offspring and, instead, help its full siblings to have theirs. Despite first appearances, this gene may be positively selected. For there is a 50 per cent chance that each full sibling also possesses this gene by common descent; and if the individual's personal reproductive loss confers sufficient reproductive gains upon its relatives, then the gene may still increase in frequency in the next generation - and that is all we mean by saying that it is positively selected. Such a gene is said to increase what the evolutionary biologist William D. Hamilton (1964) has termed the 'inclusive fitness' of the non-reproducing individual.

Kin selection is relevant to the evolution of aggression. Consider, for example, an eagle's nest containing two eaglets, Gertrude and Cecily, who are full siblings. A parent bird has just given Gertrude a tasty morsel; the question is, should Cecily take it away? A little careful thought about the idea of inclusive fitness shows that, since Gertrude contains on the average one half of Cecily's genes by common descent, natural selection will favour such behaviour only if Cecily's net gain in terms of survival is more than half of Gertrude's net cost. Thus if, as a result of being deprived of her tasty morsel, Gertrude suffers a 20 per cent drop in her chances of surviving to fledge, Cecily must enjoy a corresponding increase in her chances of surviving to fledge of more than 10 per cent in order for natural selection to favour such behaviour. This same criterion applies to the question of whether Cecily would harm her sister to the point where she was unable to feed at all.

Our analysis may perhaps explain the high level of aggression that is to be found among eaglets in a nest - a level that often leads, directly or indirectly, to the death of one sibling. At the same time, however, it provides us with some evolutionary limits to aggression between relatives. For natural selection will not favour aggressive behaviour between siblings where such behaviour gives only a small benefit to the aggressor relative to the cost suffered by the victim. Observations on Belding's ground squirrels appear to support this analysis: female ground squirrels aggressively chase and exclude intruders from their territories; but they are much more tolerant of their grown sisters and half-sisters (Sherman 1980).

Where an individual's behaviour does not affect the survival and reproduction of relatives, classical fitness and inclusive fitness are identical. Under these circumstances, we can legitimately confine our attention to the expected number of offspring produced in a lifetime. This appears to be true in the well-studied case of aggression between red deer stags. The stags disperse after weaning, but brothers do not disperse together. Thus two stags contesting with one another are unlikely to be closely related. However, given that most social groups consist in whole or in part of groups of genetic relatives, the complications of inclusive fitness must be regarded as of major importance in the evolution of social behaviour.

Taking account of what everyone else is doing

The second complication that arises in connection with the evolution of social behaviour is simply this: the fitness effects of a given social behaviour pattern depend crucially upon what other individuals are doing as well. Consider once again the example of red deer stags. Suppose that stags' antlers are primarily antipredator devices. If so, then probably the degree of protection they afford is quite closely related to size, but not (or at least, not very closely) to the size of other stags' antlers.

However, now suppose (as is more probable) that stags' antlers are not primarily antipredator but rather antistag devices, by which one individual seeks to secure mates in direct competition with another. If so, then it is immediately clear that the fitness payoffs of larger antlers depend crucially on the characteristics of other stags' antlers. A stag with 3-metre antlers may do handsomely well against rivals with 2-metre antlers, but disastrously badly against others with 4-metre antlers. Here, what matters is not how well one individual can fight, but how well one can fight in comparison with another.

This point applies generally, and its most profound consequence is that it forces us to think about fluctuations in the evolutionary fortunes of any particular behavioural trait in response to changes in the nature and frequency of other traits in the immediate social environment. Recently, evolutionary biologists have begun to tackle this issue with the help of game theories. Game theories were originally designed for any form of interactive competition or contest between human players in which there were predetermined and discoverable costs and benefits for particular interactions, and in which players were able to select alternative 'strategies' or particular ways of playing in the light of what their opponents were thought able or likely to do. Game theories specify mathematically what will be the fortunes of particular strategies when these are played against one another under specified conditions.

Transferring game theories into evolutionary biology means treating social interactions as imaginary games in which costs and benefits are defined in terms of fitness 'payoffs' resulting from the 'playing' of alternative behavioural 'strategies' one against another. Two related assumptions are made about such alternative strategies: first, it is assumed that they are traits in the sense defined above; and, secondly, it is assumed that they do not depend upon any conscious thought or intent on the part of the animal 'players'.

The single most important contribution to evolutionary game theory to date has been John Maynard Smith's idea of an evolutionarily stable strategy (see, for example, Maynard Smith 1974). A strategy is evolutionarily stable if, when most or all of a population of individuals are using it, the population cannot be successfully invaded by an alternative, mutant strategy. If there were an alternative strategy that could do better, then it would be favoured by natural selection, and there would not be stability but change. To the extent that animals in a given population are 'playing' behavioural strategies that are the long-term products of natural selection, and to the extent that a stable strategy has been both available and attainable in the course of the population's history, this is what the animals in question are expected to be playing.

The concept of an evolutionarily stable strategy provides a framework within which to analyse the natural selection of social behaviour, but it does not make our task easy. The difficulty lies in the twin possibilities, first, that there may not be a single evolutionarily stable strategy at all, or, secondly, that there may be many more than one. Where there is no stable strategy, there will be no evolutionary stability. The population will continue to evolve, either by oscillating between strategies over time, or by continually evolving in one direction (e.g., bigger and bigger stags' antlers), perhaps until some other force acts to halt the process. Perhaps, as has been suggested for the Irish elk, the species simply goes extinct.

With more than one stable strategy it becomes important to know not only the range of available strategies, together with their relevant costs and benefits, but also the history of the population under consideration. We may compare this situation with the problem of which side of the road to drive on. Driving on the left and driving on the right are both stable strategies of driving behaviour: if everyone else is driving on the left, you cannot do better than to follow suit; and the same applies if they are driving on the right. Elementary game-theoretic calculation tells us that in any particular population everyone should be doing the same thing; but it does not tell us which particular thing everyone should be doing without some additional historical information. Of course, in the case of driving the two strategies are not genetic but rather cultural alternatives; however, this does not affect the general point about situations in which there is more than one stable alternative.

An evolutionarily stable strategy is not necessarily an optimal strategy (i.e., a strategy that maximizes the fitnesses of those adopting it). It is, rather, an unbeatable strategy. It is not the best strategy, but the strategy against which one can do no better. There will be situations where the evolutionarily stable strategy corresponds to the optimal strategy. This is the case, for example, in the situation in which stags' antlers are evolving as antipredator devices. Here, both the evolutionarily stable strategy approach and the optimization approach give us the same answer. However, there are important lessons to be learnt from situations where this is not the case. One such is known as the Prisoner's Dilemma, and it is a powerful aid in thinking about the evolution of social behaviour.

The Prisoner's Dilemma

Consider two prisoners who are suspected of having committed a number of crimes. Suppose that, if they both say nothing, there will be insufficient evidence to convict either of the most serious offence, and each will escape with a relatively light sentence. If, however, one informs against the other, the authorities will set the informer free as a reward for their being able to convict the other of the most serious offence. If, on the other hand, both prisoners inform against each other, they will not be treated so kindly. The punishment for informing and at the same time being informed against will be greater than the relatively light sentence applying where both prisoners say nothing, but not so great as that for saying nothing and being incriminated by the other prisoner. Finally, let us suppose that each prisoner knows that the same terms have been offered to the other, and that each must decide what to do in ignorance of the other's decision.

		Column player	
		Cooperate	**Defect**
Row player	**Cooperate**	R=3, R=3	S=0, T=5
	Defect	T=5, S=0	P=1, P=1

Figure 8.1 The payoffs for all possible outcomes of a simple Prisoner's Dilemma game in which each player has the choice either to cooperate or to defect. Note that the payoffs to the row chooser are listed first. R = reward for mutual cooperation; S = sucker's payoff; T = temptation to defect; P = punishment for mutual defection.

This all sounds rather complicated, but it can be modelled as a very simple game between the prisoners in which each has two and only two available strategies: 'cooperate' (do not inform on the opponent); and 'defect' (inform on the opponent). The outcomes of all possible encounters are defined in terms of the relative payoffs listed above, and of course they depend upon what each player is doing. Figure 8.1 shows the results of all possible plays in a hypothetical game. The best payoff is achieved when a player defects but his opponent does not (T = 5, the 'temptation' to defect); the next best payoff is achieved when neither player defects (R = 3, the 'reward' for mutual cooperation); next comes the case when neither player cooperates (P = 1, the 'punishment' for mutual defection); and, worst of all, is the situation where a player cooperates but his opponent does not (S = 0, the 'sucker's' payoff for being exploited). It is the essence of the Prisoner's Dilemma that T is greater than R which is greater than P which is greater than S.

To see the dilemma, consider what you should do in such a game. If your opponent should happen to cooperate, you would be best off defecting (payoff = T). However, if your opponent should happen to defect, you would still be best off defecting (payoff = P, which is still better than S, your only other alternative). Irrespective of your opponent's decision, therefore, your best interest lies in defection. Now, of course, exactly the same logic applies to your opponent, so 'defect' is the one and only stable strategy for this game. In a society where everyone else is playing 'defect', you can do no better than to follow suit. The prisoners' 'dilemma' is, of course, that with everyone playing this stable strategy, the payoff to each is P = 1; whereas with everyone playing the unstable strategy 'cooperate', the payoff to each is R = 3. Here, then, cooperation is the strategy that, were everyone to adopt it, would maximize the fitness of all players; but cooperation is not the unbeatable and uncheatable strategy.

The Prisoner's Dilemma probably applies to a wide variety of real-life situations. Hamilton (1971), for example, considers the case of polygyny in birds (polygyny is the condition in which a single male may mate with several females). Let us suppose that a male may mate bigamously by usurping the territory of a neighbouring male and gaining access to one of his neighbour's females in addition to his own. An aggressive male (playing defect) that ousts a non-aggressive male (playing cooperate) will do very well (payoff = T), whereas an ousted male will do very badly (payoff = S). Two aggressive males trying to oust one another will do worse than two non-aggressive males leaving each others' females alone (payoff R is greater than P), though not so badly as a non-aggressive male ousted by an aggressive one (P is greater than S). Once again, since defection is the evolutionarily stable strategy, it seems that cooperation (in this case, non-aggression) is doomed to be eliminated.

It is worth noting that game-theoretic models are by their very nature somewhat idealistic. For purely practical reasons, game theorists are obliged to make bold assumptions about the nature of social interactions, about the strategies that may be available to players, and about the payoffs for each strategy against all others. In fact, it is often very difficult to know how realistic such assumptions may be in any particular situation; and for this reason, much evolutionary game theory tends to operate at the level of abstract thought-experiments rather than of concrete empirical research. Such thought-experiments can be very useful in helping evolutionary biologists to explore the logical possibilities that are inherent in particular kinds of social relationship. However, we should bear in mind the old computer jibe GIGO (garbage in, garbage out). If real-world behaviour does not conform to the expectations of a particular payoff matrix, so much the worse for that matrix.

Evolutionary insights into aggression

In this section we shall briefly discuss one or two important insights that Darwinism provides into behaviour in general, and aggressive behaviour in particular. This discussion will pave the way for an examination of the evolution of human conflict.

Nobody necessarily benefits from evolution

Today, most evolutionary ethologists are agreed that natural selection operates to a significant extent only on individuals, and that there is nothing in nature that 'looks out' for the good of the species. On the contrary, evolution can and often does proceed in a direction that is inimical to the species. For example, if access to mates depends upon success in combat, then the process that Darwin termed sexual selection may favour ever-escalating levels of intrasexual aggression; indeed, in this situation the members of one sex may find themselves in what has aptly been termed an evolutionary 'arms race' (Dawkins and Krebs 1979). Quite possibly, this may account for the evolution of the Irish elk's unwieldy rack of antlers and the narwhal's extraordinary tusk (Silverman and Dunbar 1980); almost certainly, it accounts for the bloody battles that take place between male elephant seals during the breeding season – battles in which newly born infants may be crushed and killed as the gigantic males strive for access to the females (Le Boeuf 1974). Clearly, sexual selection does not improve the survival prospects of the species as a whole; on the contrary, the final result of its operation may be the species' extinction.

As if this were not bad enough, we have already seen that even from the point of view of the individual things may get worse rather than better as a result of the operation of natural selection. In the case of the Prisoner's Dilemma, individuals would be better off (i.e., they would have higher individual fitnesses) if only they were not driven to the evolutionarily stable strategy from a situation in which they started out by cooperating with one another! The sobering fact is, therefore, that nobody - individual, group, or species - necessarily benefits from evolution. Sometimes an individual organism or group of organisms may be said in retrospect to have benefited from the operation of natural selection, and sometimes it may not. Either way, however, the differential propagation of genetic variants down the generations is not guaranteed to contribute to the welfare of anyone in particular.

It can pay to be very nasty

Accompanying the realization that natural selection does not take account of the welfare of groups or species, there has been a growing recognition in recent years that individual selection may generate extremely aggressive behaviour between members of the same species. For example, there is now a significant number of field reports of intraspecific killing (for a partial review, see Hausfater and Hrdy 1984). For the most part, the victims of such killing appear to be young individuals; but a number of studies have documented that adults too may suffer serious and even fatal injuries as a result of intraspecific fighting (Wilson 1975). In red deer, for example, 5–10 per cent of stags suffer serious or fatal injuries (Clutton-Brock, Guinness, and Albon 1982).

Hand in hand with this appreciation that the most extreme forms of aggression can occur between members of the same species, there has gone a radical reinterpretation of those many cases in which intraspecific aggression is undoubtedly far more restrained. It was the 'gloved fist' appearance of many animal contests that so impressed Konrad Lorenz, who interpreted the phenomenon as an adaptation for the good of the species. However, evolutionary game theory has shown that a certain amount of restraint may often be in an individual aggressor's best interests (Maynard Smith 1974). In particular, wherever the cost of injury in a contest is greater than the benefit of winning (and this is probably a common situation), the extremely aggressive strategy 'hawk' (always fight until either you win or you are injured) is not stable. Here, then, is a possibility for the explanation of 'gloved fist' strategies without recourse to Lorenzian arguments about the good of the species.

The picture that is emerging today from both theoretical and empirical research on the evolution of animal aggression is, in part at least, a sober one. Where extremely aggressive strategies have been available, and where they have increased individuals' inclusive fitnesses, it appears that they have evolved; and this, irrespective of whether the individuals involved are members of the same or a different species, of whether they are related or unrelated, known or unknown, young or old. Clearly, nature can indeed be very nasty.

It can also pay to be very nice

Despite what has just been said, evolutionary theory indicates at least three factors that may act to limit the aggressiveness of social interactions. The first is, as we saw in the 'gloved fist' example above, that there may be nothing whatever to be gained from it. Very often, animals can gain direct personal benefits from relatively non-aggressive interactions. Assuming, however, that there is at least some potential personal benefit to be gained from aggression, this must be set against a second limiting factor, which has already been discussed – namely, the possibility that the two contestants are genetically related. As we have seen, inclusive fitness considerations will restrain aggression wherever the (classical fitness) benefits to the aggressor are insufficient to outway the (inclusive fitness) costs of his or her aggression; and such inclusive fitness costs can, of course, be considerable.

The third limitation on aggression involves the possibility that two potential aggressors may meet up again in the future. This point may be illustrated with reference to the Prisoner's Dilemma. As explained earlier, this dilemma arises in encounters between individuals where, although both could do well by cooperating, neither can afford to do because of the risk of being cheated by the other. But what if there are opportunities for repeated encounters between the same players? Robert Axelrod and William Hamilton (1981) have shown that, if the probability that two players will meet again is high, and if each can remember the behaviour of the other in the last encounter, then a strategy less selfish than 'always defect' may be stable. This strategy is 'cooperate on the first encounter, and thereafter do whatever your opponent did last'; or, more simply, 'tit-for-tat'.

Some of the significant features of this simple strategy are worth noting. First, tit-for-tat always starts by acting cooperatively (that is, non-aggressively), and it always maintains this stance so long as an opponent reciprocates. Secondly, tit-for-tat always 'punishes' defection with an immediate defection of its own; but it only requires that the opponent switch to cooperation for tit-for-tat to 'reward' such behaviour by reverting to cooperation – in Axelrod and Hamilton's phrase, tit-for-tat is very 'forgiving'. Thirdly, by virtue of being simple (and therefore easy to 'understand'), consistent, and continually forgiving, tit-for-tat gives its opponent every incentive to benefit in repeated encounters from the relatively high reward score for mutual cooperation (R = 3), without risk of incurring the penalty of the sucker's payoff (S = 0).

This last point is the key to tit-for-tat's extraordinary success in both rounds of an open-entry international computer tournament set up by Robert Axelrod, in which entrants were invited to submit strategies for an each-against-all iterated Prisoner's Dilemma game. Tit-for-tat won the first round convincingly; but, far more remarkably, it also won the second round, even though on this occasion mathematicians, evolutionary biologists, and others were able to use the results of the first round in devising new and often very sophisticated counter-strategies (Axelrod 1984)!

We shall return to this result later on. For the moment, let it simply be said that this development within game theory demonstrates that, in principle at least, the evolutionary process contains quite as much potentiality for the development of cooperative social relationships as it does for the development of competitive ones. It is too early to say how much actual tit-for-tat behaviour empirical research will reveal, though already we note that tree swallows and vampire bats appear to use tit-for-tat in interactions with one another (Lombardo 1985; Trivers 1985). In the meantime, however, it is to be hoped that the popularizers of evolution will be as quick to latch on to this exciting area of inquiry as they have been in the past to boast of the nastier works of nature.

Variability is important

In the early days, ethology focused a great deal of attention on species-typical behaviour. Contemporary evolutionary ethology, on the other hand, has shifted the spotlight away from what all individuals in a species always do and towards the interesting differences that may exist both between individuals and within the same individual at different times. Just as natural selection may not favour behaviour that benefits individuals, so it may not favour the same behaviour in all individuals, or even the same behaviour in the same individual all the time.

Given a population of competing stags, we have already seen that we must look at significant differences between them before we can assess the benefit of having antlers of any particular size. Equally, however, where a majority of stags are caught up in an evolutionary 'arms race' that is generating ever larger antlers and ever higher levels of aggressiveness, natural selection may favour individuals who drop out of the conventional competition altogether and opt for what are commonly referred to as 'sneaky' mating strategies. This may explain the presence in red deer populations of antler-less stags, or 'hummels' (Clutton-Brock, Guinness, and Albon 1982).

There are two fundamentally different methods by which alternative forms of behaviour can evolve. On the one hand, individuals may possess what are termed conditional strategies, such that they behave one way in one set of conditions and another way in a different set; and on the other, they may use mixed strategies, such that one of two or more alternate forms of behaviour may be employed with a certain probability in a single set of conditions.

Both methods are believed to exist in nature. In the bee *Centris pallada*, for example, males emerging from pupation appear to adopt as a method of finding a mate the conditional strategy, 'if large, patrol and fight over emerging females; if small, hover and attempt to mate with females not guarded by patrollers'. In the digger wasp *Sphex ichneumoneus*, on the other hand, females appear to adopt the mixed strategy, 'dig your own burrow with probability P; enter someone else's burrow with probability $(1 - P)$'; with the value of P being fixed such that the two alternatives have approximately equal reproductive success (Brockmann, Grafen, and Dawkins 1979).

We hope that enough has now been said to lay to rest the notion, still found even in some quite recent ethological textbooks (see, for example, Eibl-Eibesfeldt 1978), that the biological components of behaviour are the universal, species-specific ones. Biology is as full of subtle diversity and variability as any culture. This discovery may yet come to be seen as one of the greatest achievements of contemporary evolutionary ethology.

Natural selection cannot explain everything

For all its undoubted power, natural selection cannot explain every aspect of behaviour. For one thing, it is unlikely that all traits can be selected independently of one another. For example, selection for speed of running to escape from predators may prevent selection for strength to overcome competitors; and in this situation, single-trait analysis will not suffice. In addition, there may be other forces at work in the evolution of behaviour besides natural selection. Chance, for example, plays its part in the evolution of behaviour, as it does in the evolution of everything else. Finally, and most important of all, it is necessary to take account of the role of learning, and particularly of cultural tradition.

Some care is needed if the problem presented to the evolutionary biologist by learning is to be stated correctly. Learning abilities themselves can, of course, be traits subject to the influence of natural selection. For example, laboratory rats learn to associate a novel taste with subsequent nausea after only one trial, whereas they experience considerable difficulty with other similar associations – such as, for example, that between a novel taste and an electric shock, or that between a novel visual stimulus and subsequent nausea (Shettleworth 1984). Clearly, the rat's particular learning ability is useful to it in the wild, where new foods may well kill by poisoning but are unlikely to do so by electrocution; and it seems reasonable to suppose that this ability is the product of evolution by natural selection.

Let us grant, therefore, that natural selection can endow animals with specific learning abilities. However, it cannot dictate in advance the entire range of uses to which such abilities will be put. Perhaps animals will use their learning abilities to do those things for the sake of which those abilities evolved in the first place; but then again, perhaps they will not. Either way, it is easy to see that a certain indeterminacy or openendedness is introduced into behaviour once the evolutionary process has endowed animals with powerful learning abilities; and it is this openendedness that may cause problems when we come to reconstruct the evolution of observed behaviour.

To take a somewhat trivial example, consider the way in which parrots mimic sounds. Suppose (as seems probable) that this is an evolved adaptation, favoured by natural selection in order to enable parrots to learn their species-specific song, or some local dialect of their species-specific song, or even the song of some other species altogether. Of course, this is all supposition; but it is perfectly plausible supposition. What is perfectly implausible, however, is that natural selection has endowed parrots with their extraordinary learning abilities in order that they should be able to sing 'Who's a pretty boy, then?'. Yet this is precisely what many parrots now learn with the aid of their remarkable gift. Natural selection has, as it were, been foiled by one of its own inventions.

What is true in a minor way of parrots is true in a major way of primates, and particularly of humans. In our own case, evolved learning abilities are so extensive that they have given rise to a largely autonomous and extremely rapid process of what is sometimes (and rather misleadingly) termed 'cultural evolution'. The really important point here is that the cumulative and runaway processes of behaviour modification going on all around us in our own societies are at once perfectly consistent with and yet almost entirely independent of the Darwinian processes of genetic variation and selection. They are perfectly consistent with Darwinism in the sense that everything we learn – from our language to our car licence-number – is made possible by our evolved learning abilities; and yet they are almost entirely independent of

Darwinian processes in the sense that the relationship between our evolved learning abilities and much of what we know is similar to the relationship between a parrot's ability to mimic sounds and its singing 'Who's a pretty boy, then?'.

Of course, some of the things we know (e.g., a language) may well represent evolved behavioural adaptations. Moreover, we must not forget that Darwinian evolution still grinds on regardless within human populations; and it is perfectly possible (though in most cases it is of little or no practical consequence) that genetic differences between individuals with respect to learning abilities continue to accumulate in particular (and largely unknown) directions under the influence of natural selection.

These qualifications, however, are beside the point, which is that we must always be careful to distinguish those cases where it is appropriate to ask Darwinian questions from those where it is not. Altogether too much of what passes in the literature for human evolutionary ethology takes the form of highly ingenious answers to questions of the general type: why has natural selection favoured genetically variant parrots that tend to sing 'Who's a pretty boy, then?' whenever someone comes into the room? The only sensible answer to this question is that it hasn't. Even the most ardent advocate of the extreme Darwinian thesis that natural selection is all in evolution must recognize that there are limits to what it can reasonably be asked to explain.

The evolution of human conflict

How far will evolutionary theory take us in our understanding of the science and politics of human conflict? Strong claims have been made here, both among Lorenzian ethologists and among those who belong to the modern, 'sociobiological' school of evolutionary ethology. With but a single exception, however (of which more in a moment), we shall not consider these claims in any detail here. In each case, the reasons for this decision are easily stated. As was explained at some length in Chapters 3, 7, and earlier in this chapter, the theoretical foundations of Lorenzian ethology are extremely shaky – so shaky, in fact, that its superstructure of conclusions concerning human behaviour requires complete demolition, not close inspection with a view to minor maintenance and repairs.

So far as the modern school is concerned, most of its strong claims to date concerning human behaviour have fallen into one of three equally unsatisfactory categories: (1) grand-sounding but extremely vague pronouncements that look more like promisory notes than workable hypotheses (Wilson 1978; Alexander 1979); (2) even more grand-sounding and highly mathematicized formulations that turn out on closer inspection to have exactly the same weaknesses as the promisory notes (Lumsden and Wilson 1981; Maynard Smith and Warren 1982; Kitcher 1985); and (3) highly detailed empirical studies of particular practices, such as axe fights among South American Indians (Chagnon and Bugos 1979) or female infanticide in traditional Hindu societies (Dickemann 1979), whose sheer confinement in cultural space and time strongly suggests that they cannot possibly be the specific products of evolution by natural selection (Kitcher 1985).

Leaving aside, therefore, the bulk of the existing literature, let us consider afresh two quite different methods of applying evolutionary theory that, in principle at least, might offer useful insights into human conflict. The first method involves inquiry into the history of the higher primates in general, and the hominids in particular, with a view to discovering a set of evolved behavioural adaptations that we inherit from our common ancestors. If successful, such an undertaking would both define a number of specific behavioural dispositions or tendencies possessed by some or all humans today, and explain how these had evolved into human populations living in their ancestral environment(s). Moreover, this undertaking might even be able to make interesting and worthwhile points about the biological and social effects of these evolved traits in the wide variety of altered environments in which humans live today.

All this, a completely successful inquiry into hominid behavioural evolution could, in principle, deliver. In practice, however, achieving complete (or even moderate) success in such an inquiry is extremely difficult. As was pointed out in Chapter 4, we are ignorant of almost all of the relevant factors that would be necessary in order to discover the relevant set of ancestral hominid behavioural adaptations. At a time when we cannot even specify the detailed physical ecology of the early hominids, let alone make accurate predictions about their detailed behaviour, we are left with either the second-best option of indirect and probably misleading analogies with other species or the third-rate option of rank and unbridled speculation. Those with little taste for either of these activities will prefer to postpone this inquiry pending the development of a much fuller and richer account of hominid evolution than is currently available.

The second approach to the subject is quite different, and at least a little less difficult. It consists in the attempt to make use of our relatively secure body of theoretical knowledge about the evolution of behaviour in general to explore the nature and potential of particular kinds of human relationship more fully than might otherwise have been possible. This undertaking is worthwhile, not only because it highlights some of the ways in which human behaviour is and is not similar to the behaviour of other animals, but also because it fosters a spirit at once positive and critical towards the possibility that biology may contain useful lessons for human society. Without either accepting the findings of evolutionary ethology wholesale as the solution to human ills, or rejecting them wholesale as irrelevant to creatures so sublime as ourselves, this approach invites us to be highly selective in what we take from evolutionary ethology by way of insights into the human condition.

The area where this approach appears most promising at the moment is evolutionary game theory. This is hardly to be wondered at. After all, game theory was originally developed as a device for modelling human behaviour; and since it was borrowed by evolutionary biologists for a slightly different purpose, it has undergone something of a renaissance. John Maynard Smith has suggested that it would be appropriate if, having borrowed game theory from the social sciences, biologists were to return it 'somewhat sharpened up' (Maynard Smith 1983). What are the prospects, then, for new insights into human behaviour from evolutionary game theory?

Before answering this question, it is important to enter a major qualification concerning the nature of game theory. As has already been pointed out, the essence of the game-theoretic approach to behaviour is strategic, not genetic. The crucial thing about a game is that there be a number of alternative behavioural strategies playing against one another. Whether these strategies are the result of reasoning on the part of animals blessed with foresight and intelligence, on the one hand, or of natural selection among animals without the gift of reason, on the other, is from the point of view of game theory a matter of complete indifference.

In the case of other animals Darwinism requires us to assume that alternative strategies are traits in the biological sense defined earlier; but in our own case, this assumption no longer makes good sense. For we know that humans are capable of devising their own behavioural strategies – how else would they have invented game theory? Thus, the simplest hypothesis regarding a great deal of human 'game-playing' behaviour is that alternative strategies are the result of what economists sometimes refer to rather grandly as 'the rational calculation of self-interest' – or, more probably, of some considerably muddier social-psychological equivalent.

This is a cause, not for despondency, but rather for taking pains to be clear about the kinds of games that we are playing. Let us suppose that we wish to construct a game-theoretic model of human conflict. The question arises: is this a biological model, involving competition between alternative genetic strategies within an evolving population; or is it a psychological model, involving competition between alternative rational strategies within a particular human culture? If the model is biological, then at least the situation is theoretically unambiguous: strategies will succeed or fail as they contribute to the inclusive fitnesses of individuals playing them. If the model is psychological, however, then things are far less clear. In this case, presumably, strategies will succeed or fail as they are judged to be effective in achieving individuals' interests; but here, as Kitcher (1985) has pointed out, there is no reason whatever to expect these interests to be confined to the maximization of reproductive success.

It is in this qualification about the nature of the games people play that there lie the seeds of the one really major difficulty confronting those who wish to apply evolutionary game theory to human behaviour. It is a striking fact about game theory that it appears to be more powerful in its (secondary) applications to evolving organisms than it ever was in its (primary) applications to game-playing people. A key reason for this is as follows: in order to apply game theory in any particular situation, we must be able to construct payoff matrices of the kind illustrated in Figure 8.1 (see p. 130). However, in order to construct payoff matrices we must be able to specify the costs and benefits accruing to any particular strategy when played against any other; and in order to specify these costs and benefits, we must be able to define each player's self-interest – to decide, in other words, what it is that each player wishes to get out of the game.

The great virtue of our (secondary) applications of game theory to evolving organisms is that they operate with a clear and unambiguous criterion by which to judge what each 'player' in a game 'wishes' to get out of it. For we know from first principles that animal 'players' are to be regarded (metaphorically, of course) as 'trying' to maximize their inclusive fitnesses in social interactions. Once we abandon the evolutionary process for games based on foresight and rational calculation, however, we lose this clear and unambiguous criterion of self-interest. When we are dealing with humans engaged in even the most apparently straightforward of social interactions, it is far from obvious what the individual 'players' in the putative 'game' may be trying to maximize. In selling their labour in the labour market, for example, are potential employees trying to maximize their income, their pleasure, their self-esteem, their welfare, their family's welfare, or what? No mathematical formula will tell us the answer to this and myriad similar questions that bedevil game-theoretic approaches within the social sciences.

Here, then, is the source of the difficulty. Evolutionary game theories work well precisely because they eliminate all possible ends or goals for social behaviour except that of maximizing inclusive fitness; but as soon as we wish to cash in the successes of these theories in the domain of human behaviour, back comes the extraordinary plurality of ends or goals that humans are capable of devising for themselves. Somehow or other (and we have already noted our ignorance on this count), natural selection has endowed us all with the most marvellously complex psychologies, by virtue of which it is abundantly obvious that we can and do conceive the most extraordinarily varied interests and purposes in life. To the extent that these varied interests are at stake in the 'games' that we play, they must be taken into account before game theory can be rigorously applied.

This point has been recognized quite widely in the literature. Thus, Maynard Smith (1983) notes that, in the case of human behaviour, 'instead of seeking evolutionarily stable states, we have to seek states which are stable if behaviour is determined by perceived self-interest, subject to custom and to legal constraints'. Well and good; but where is the comprehensive social-psychological theory that will vouchsafe reliable verdicts concerning the perceived self-interest of human actors involved in potentially aggressive (or any other kind of) social interactions under the combined influence of custom and legal constraints? What, for example, was the perceived self-interest of young recruits in the trenches during the First World War? Was it to stay alive at all costs, to take 'reasonable' risks (whatever they may have been) in the service of their country, or to die gloriously in a noble cause? Perhaps some psychology of the remote future may solve such problems with ease; but at present we are so far from this happy eventuality that we cannot discern even the dim outlines of what such a solution may be.

We conclude, then, that in spite of the number, range, and comparative successfulness of the recent developments that have taken place in evolutionary game theory as applied to animal behaviour, the prospects for the rigorous application of this body of theory to contemporary human social behaviour remain rather poor. Does this mean, therefore, that we should abandon the hope of gleaning useful insights into human behaviour from this direction? We think not. For although we may not be able to generate testable game-theoretic predictions concerning what people will and will not do in any particular social circumstances, this need not prevent us from applying theory in the other way that has proved so valuable within evolutionary ethology; namely, as a way of exploring the logical possibilities inherent in those particular social circumstances.

Here, it would be hard indeed to better the example set by Robert Axelrod. In *The Evolution of Cooperation* (1984), Axelrod sets out the remarkable results of his two-round iterated Prisoner's Dilemma computer tournament, and draws out their implications for an understanding of the conditions under which cooperation may emerge in games between egoistic players without the aid of a central authority. His discussion makes compelling reading, and it is extensively illustrated with human behavioural examples that include, interestingly, an entire chapter on the behaviour of front-line soldiers in the First World War. The point we wish to make about this discussion here is that it is in no sense a rigorous treatment of human behaviour – there are no formal models of the behaviour of any but purely imaginary egoists, and there is no controlled data by which such models may be tested against reality – and yet this does not prevent Axelrod either from interpreting real-life human interactions or from offering extensive advice on the fostering of human cooperation.

Axelrod's success results from his decision to treat the iterated Prisoner's Dilemma as a thought-experiment. He uses it both to display the logical possibilities contained within a particular type of social relationship and to discover some simple rules by which actors who find themselves within such relationships, and administrators who wish to manipulate them, can tip the scales of probability in favour of one possibility rather than another. If you are in an iterated Prisoner's Dilemma, he suggests, you can help yourself (and, indirectly, your opponent) to benefit from the reward for mutual cooperation by: not being envious; not being the first to defect; reciprocating both cooperation and defection; and not being too clever. Similarly, if you wish to foster cooperative outcomes to iterated Prisoner's Dilemmas around you, then you should: enlarge the shadow of the future (i.e., make the future more important relative to the present); change the payoffs (e.g., increase the penalties for defection); teach people to care about each other; teach reciprocity; and improve recognition possibilities (e.g., improve the detection rate for defections).

Interestingly, this advice is a mixture of the psychological and the strategic. By taking seriously the idea that people can be taught a set of psychological attitudes that will promote cooperative outcomes to social interactions, Axelrod makes it clear that the human games with which he is concerned involve strategies of foresight and rational calculation, not of genetic variation and natural selection; and at the same time, he makes it clear that self-interest is not the only criterion by which such strategies may be devised. For if people can be taught a concern for others that will foster more cooperative behaviour, then it must be possible to change the ends or goals that they seek in social intercourse. Nor is it enough to say, as Axelrod does, that, 'If a sister is concerned for the welfare of her brother, the sister's self-interest can be thought of as including (among many other things) this concern for the welfare of her brother'. Either people are psychological egoists, or they are not; and if they can be made to feel concern about the welfare of others to the point where personal interests may be compromised, then clearly they are not always and inevitably psychological egoists.

This last point merely confirms the status of the Prisoner's Dilemma as a very useful thought-experiment rather than a plausible model of real-world human behaviour. Axelrod's work is challenging for two reasons: first, it shows that real possibilities exist for non-aggression within all iterated Prisoner's Dilemmas, be they between bacteria, buffaloes, or business people; and, secondly, it shows that real possibilities exist for influencing the probability of non-aggressive outcomes to iterated Prisoner's Dilemmas when those caught up in them are not genetically evolving organisms but, rather, rational people.

It is a long way from the evolution of 'instinctive aggression' to the evolution of behavioural strategies of social conflict. The study of the evolution of conflict is today an actively growing field, and it has excited a mass of speculation about the nature and significance of aggressive interactions within human society. Nevertheless, amidst all the successes of new research, and all the wonder about their possible relevance to our own species, it is worth remembering that it is only about 20 years since ethologists learnt how questions about the evolution of social behaviour ought properly to be asked. In this chapter, we have examined the chief implications of these questions for our understanding of the evolutionary process, and explored how these implications may in the future be extended into the domain of human affairs.

Unfortunately, the sober prospects for success in this field are almost exactly opposite to the amount of public interest each tends to excite. Thus, the prospects for a genuine theory of the evolutionary 'limits' to human nature are virtually zero, even though the theme of our enslavement to our natures appears almost endlessly popular. Similarly, the prospects for a genuine theory of hominid behavioural evolution, though rather better, are still dim; and this despite the fact that it is surely behaviour rather than bones that fuels continuing public interest in palaeoanthropology.

Only in the field of the game-theoretic modelling of social behaviour do we detect signs that really useful insights into human conflict may be to hand; but, ironically, these insights appear to be quite the reverse of what the general public has long been conditioned to expect. For instead of showing yet again how 'beastly' we can be, game theory is beginning to show just how many possibilities there may be for the evolution, not of human conflict, but rather of human cooperation.

CHAPTER NINE

Aggression revisited

The naturalization of human conflict

We began this book with a brief account of the way in which an entire field of scientific inquiry grew up in the 1960s and 1970s. We suggested that the rapid increase in research on aggression in this period was in part a reflection of concrete social and political concerns, and that these concerns left their mark on the field in the form of popular cultural assumptions about the nature and significance of aggressive behaviour. Building upon a major tradition of thought about human nature in western culture, many ethologists, psychologists, psychiatrists, and sociologists came to believe that human conflict was the direct result of an aggressive 'instinct' inherited from a long line of animal ancestors. 'Beastly' behaviour was caused by 'the beast within', and the task of those who wished to promote a more peaceable world was to domesticate or tame human nature. This message was widely popularized in books and articles on the 'biological basis' of aggression; and in this way, science in turn fed back into popular culture, often confirming the very assumptions upon which it had been constructed in the first place.

During the past 20 years, our culture and our science have changed in many ways, some of which have made it easier to challenge older ways of thinking about aggression. For example, there has been an increase in awareness about the possibilities of misusing science. From the rise of the environmental movement and the birth of 'green politics' to the emergence of a critical perspective on modern medicine and the growth of 'antipsychiatry' there have been calls for the practice of more socially responsible science. Such calls reflect a climate of increasing scepticism about the wholesale application of science and technology to society; in this climate, research on aggression has come in for its fair share of critical attention.

Nevertheless, violence is still with us; and there is continuing and widespread public concern over both its causes and its possible cures. At the same time, aggression research continues apace; and, as in the 1960s and 1970s, much of this research continues to feed off and, in turn, to reinforce popular cultural presumptions about human nature. Still today, there exists a strong temptation to naturalize human conflict – that is, to portray 'aggression' as an essentially unmodifiable biological 'given' of human existence. Before reviewing how far we have come in our criticism of this view, it is worth reminding ourselves of its continuing influence. By reviewing very briefly one or two recent studies of rape, infanticide, and crime we shall see how the traditional stereotypes surrounding the biological study of human behaviour still affect the way some scientists think about aggression.

Rape

Rape has come in for a considerable amount of sociobiological discussion in recent years (e.g., Thornhill 1980; Thornhill and Thornhill 1983; Shields and Shields 1983). Predictably enough, the subject is extremely controversial; and biological interpretations have provoked stern criticism in some quarters (see, for example, Sunday and Tobach 1985). As usual in such cases, proponents on both sides of the dispute have claimed that an evolutionary analysis somehow makes rape inevitable and/or justifiable., In fact, of course, it does neither of these things; but here, as elsewhere, sociobiologists and their critics often appear to be confused about just what an evolutionary analysis implies for our understanding of human behaviour.

Thus, W.M. Shields and L.M. Shields (1983) use the fact that psychological profiles of rapists are essentially indistinguishable from those of non-rapists to support the view that the propensity to rape is universally present in normal human males as an evolved behavioural adaptation. Under appropriate reproductive cost/benefit conditions, they suggest, any normal man is likely to commit rape. From this, they conclude that social policies such as reducing sexism and rehabilitating rapists are unlikely to alter the tendency to rape; only increasing the probability and the severity of punishment (and, perhaps, decreasing the vulnerability of women) stands any real chance of success. Eventually, they point out, severe punishment would artifically select for men with higher rape thresholds, thus reducing the genetic tendency to rape in the population.

The important thing about this model is that it embodies the assumption that the propensity to rape is 'hard-wired'. Shields and Shields state, for example, that the development of this propensity is 'probably recalcitrant to reprogramming via individual experience'. Significantly, they do not even consider the possibility that the tendency to rape may depend upon particular developmental (including social) circumstances even though such a possibility is both intuitively plausible and perfectly consistent with their chosen evolutionary hypothesis.

Now, obviously, one can build into one's scientific models any assumptions one likes; but in the present case the assumption of developmental fixity is completely gratuitous. Certainly, we may be grateful to Shields and Shields for at least making this assumption explicit (all too often in the literature, it passes without mention). However, it is a pity that they should have fallen into this habitual way of thinking about a biological perspective on human affairs; for, of course, the result is that their work encourages the single most common popular misconception about such a perspective – namely, that it concerns only those things about us which cannot easily be changed or prevented.

Infanticide

A second and slightly different example from the recent sociobiological literature concerns infanticide. In the past, the killing of infants by adults of the same species has been viewed as aberrant or even 'pathological' behaviour. However, in recent years sociobiologists have had considerable success in interpreting this phenomenon within the general framework of evolutionary social theory (Hausfater and Hrdy 1984). At the heart of this interpretive effort has been the concept of conflict between the reproductive interests of females and males. It has been argued, for example, that it may be in a female's reproductive interests to postpone getting pregnant again until her last infant is fully weaned; but that, if she should acquire a new partner, it may be in his reproductive interests to kill this infant, of which he is not the father, in order to induce his potential mate to become sexually receptive to him.

In his book *Sociobiology and the Law* (1985), John Beckstrom concludes from scenarios such as this that children are more at risk of injury or death from stepfathers than from biological fathers; and he backs up this claim with statistics on human child abuse. Beckstrom considers two possible legal responses to this finding. First, perhaps milder penalties should be mandatory for men who harm or kill unrelated children, on the grounds of diminished responsibility in the face of a biological predisposition. Alternatively, perhaps tougher penalties should be imposed in such cases on the assumption that a stronger threat is required to deter a stronger biological urge to commit the offence.

It is to Beckstrom's credit that he does not claim that sociobiology can resolve the difficult and venerable issue of punishment versus deterrence in the law. But why, we may ask, does he suppose that sociobiology is relevant to the issue at all? Always assuming that his claims concerning the pattern of human child abuse and infanticide are valid, we may be able to calculate the relative probabilities of children being injured or killed by biological fathers and stepfathers in a specified range of environments; and always assuming that we know something about the development of the traits in question, then we may be able to generalize these probabilities to cover many or even most situations. At this point, sociobiology has played no part in our analysis; and yet, having got this far, what more could it possibly add that would be relevant to the moral, political, and legal issues that remain to be decided? Once we know what the facts of child abuse are, it is surely time to hand the matter over to the political and/or the judicial processes to determine what should be done about them.

There is just one way in which many people may be inclined to see sociobiology as having particular relevance in the legal setting. For when a particular behaviour pattern is interpreted biologically, it is sometimes claimed that the role of human will, and therefore the notion of personal responsibility, are thereby imperilled. This claim may then be countered by critics who maintain that the behaviour pattern is not biological at all, but rather learned; the implication being that, if this is so, the notions of will and responsibility are thereby saved.

Before entering the fray at this level, however, it may be wise to reflect upon the multiple confusions involved in this way of thinking. For not only is the dichotomy between biology and learning false, but also it does not map neatly onto the distinction between constraint and freedom. Genetic causes are not in principle any more of a threat to our notions of personal responsibility than are environmental ones (who, after all, would wish to exempt a child from responsibility for its parents' genes but blame it for its early home environment?). If the law has a problem with the notion of scientific explanations of human conduct, it is not with the invoking of genetic as opposed to environmental causes of behaviour, but rather with the invoking of any causes of behaviour whatsoever apart from the free and sovereign exercise of the will.

Crime

Moving away from sociobiology, we may consider very briefly one last example, drawn from criminologist James Q. Wilson and psychologist Richard J. Herrnstein's recent book *Crime and Human Nature* (1985). Citing a variety of studies, including work on the XYY anomaly that was discussed in Chapter 1, these authors claim that the existence of individual differences in 'biological predispositions' to criminality means 'that circumstances that activate criminal behaviour in one person will not do so in another, that social forces cannot deter criminal behaviour in 100 percent of a population'. Now the second part of this statement may be true or false (how could we possibly know?), but it does not follow from the first. Once again, we are faced with the gratuitous association of the biological with the developmentally fixed. None of the behaviour genetics data cited by Wilson and Herrnstein can legitimately be used to support this association.

The taming of biology?

Much of this book has been taken up with the attempt to expose the multiple scientific weaknesses inherent within these sorts of interpretations of biology. To some readers, this may have seemed at the outset a needless exercise. Do not essentially all modern behavioural biologists agree, these readers may have been inclined to ask, that the old nature/nurture dispute is dead and gone? It is to be hoped that anyone who thought this way at the outset will by now have been persuaded to think again. For notwithstanding all the protestations that routinely accompany the publication of papers and books on the biology of behaviour, the terms of the old nature/nurture dispute stubbornly refuse to go away. Somehow or another, many biologists and social scientists seem still to gravitate to the distinction between a biological core of fixed and a cultural overlay of flexible behavioural attributes.

The way in which old and supposedly outdated modes of thought survive in modern analyses of animal and human behaviour has been analysed interestingly by the American anthropologist and political scientist Dafydd Greenwood (1984). According to Greenwood, there have been in the western world for fully two millennia only 'a small set of recipes for biocultural arguments'. Most of these recipes, he suggests, have their origins in the classical doctrine that each object in nature possesses an ideal specific form. In the classical doctrine of the four 'humors', for example, each species of living thing has essentially distinct qualities by virtue of having a unique combination of humors. Humors are acquired genealogically (typically, through 'blood lines'), and environmentally (typically, through the influence of local place); and it becomes a matter of empirical inquiry to determine how much of each influence - nature versus nurture - is involved in the generation of a particular species' character, temperament, or 'humor'.

The world view within which the doctrine of the four humors made sense was providential, hierarchical, and static. There were fixed temperaments in nature because nature was a divinely instituted economy in which there was a fixed place for everything and everything was in its place. This world view is supposed to have collapsed, of course, in the mid-nineteenth century. In the Darwinian universe, after all, there was no guarantee of providential order, natural hierarchy, or biological stasis. For Darwin, individual variation was a central fact of life; and species possessed no essential or ideal natures at all. On this view, then, Darwinism ought to have ended the quest for a fixed human nature, in opposition to human nurture, once and for all.

Instead, however, Greenwood argues that Darwinism was 'tamed' by the older vision. Rather than departing radically from pre-evolutionary modes of thought, succeeding generations of supposedly Darwinian scientists simply rewrote traditional schemes within a framework that was only superficially modern. Thus, traditional typologies were revamped in the late nineteenth century as supposedly temporal series; and over and again, old constitutional and racial distinctions based upon the notion of essential forms were given a mere evolutionary gloss. Greenwood suggests that even many modern studies of the 'biological basis' of human behaviour remain fundamentally humoralist, in the sense that they continue to operate with the old, pre-Darwinian distinctions of nature and nurture, constraint and freedom. etc. Despite all appearances, for example, he insists that E. O. Wilson's (1978) sociobiological quest for an understanding of our fixed biological nature has been 'fully domesticated by an ancient western cultural vision'.

The decline of aggression?

The myth of the beast within fits perfectly Greenwood's model of a pre-evolutionary idea that has lived on in pseudo-Darwinian guise. Having no legitimate basis in modern genetics and evolutionary theory, the myth remains plausible precisely because it closely resembles and strongly supports a major thread in the history of western thought, a thread that we have traced from the Christian doctrine of human nature, through the Hobbesian doctrine of human society as a continual war of each against all, and on into a number of the most influential philosophies of human nature in the twentieth century. In modern times, of course, the myth has gained considerably in cultural authority by virtue of its supposedly scientific status.

We have detected the influence of this myth upon biological investigations of aggressive behaviour in several areas. First, there was the misleading assumption that aggression is a natural category, whether for purposes of causal, developmental, functional, or evolutionary analysis; secondly, there was the continuing and largely sterile obsession with defining the separate contributions of nature and nurture to aggression; thirdly, there was the misguided and unproductive determination to locate aggression in particular genes, hormones, or 'brain centres'; and, fourthly, there was the unjustified assumption that aggression is an 'innate' and unalterable feature of human existence.

On each of these counts we have argued that the evidence is all against the notion of the beast within. First, aggression is not a natural category of analysis; rather, it is a more-or-less useful construct that we impose upon nature for our own (more-or-less) sensible purposes. Secondly, aggression cannot be parcelled out to nature or nurture, or even to some combination of a biological 'core' of impulses and a cultural 'overlay' of modifiers or constraints. Thirdly, aggression is not 'located' in particular genes, hormones, or brain 'centres'; rather, various kinds of aggressive behaviour are the developmental consequences in specific environments of multiple and diverse interactions within and between social animals or humans. Fourthly, aggressive behaviour is not unalterable; on the contrary, it is one of the most flexible and widely varying aspects of the social lives of animals and people.

If this view of animal and human conflict is accepted, it is hard to avoid the conclusion that the field of aggression research has a largely spurious identity. 'Aggression' is not a single thing, nor yet a single class of things; it is not a single behaviour pattern, nor yet a single class of behaviour patterns; rather, it is a single term, with a great variety of possible uses and misuses. Already, we detect signs in the literature that the spotlight of scientific attention is beginning to turn away from this term. Behavioural ecologists have begun to explore not so much the evolution of 'aggression' as the evolution of 'conflict'; and even this category is beginning to dissolve, as social interactions come to be seen as characteristically involving complex blends of conflict and cooperation. Similarly, students of motivation have largely abandoned the attempt to model aggression as an instinct, or indeed as a single motivational system of any sort; and instead, attention has shifted to the analysis of more functionally specific behaviour patterns. The field of aggression research shows signs of splitting up.

If this is so, it will not be the first (or the last) time that such a thing has happened in the behavioural sciences. To the phrenologists of the early nineteenth century, for example, it seemed obvious that behaviour was to be understood in terms of discrete mental faculties and instincts (including, in Franz Gall's original scheme, 'self-defence and courage' and 'carnivorous instinct, tendency to murder', and in later elaborations both 'combativeness' and 'destructiveness'; but not, interestingly, 'aggression'). To the brain scientists of the late nineteenth century, however, most of these faculties and instincts appeared quite useless as starting points for investigating the relationship between brain and mind. Perhaps in years to come, behavioural scientists will look back on the mid-twentieth century preoccupation with 'aggression' in exactly the same way that we look back today upon so many of the phrenologists' faculties.

Can biology be made to tell a different story?

We have a long way still to go in reformulating our ideas about the biological and the social worlds. Still today, the old stereotypes inform scientific and popular writings about animal and human behaviour. That they have an effect on the views of those who are on the outside of biology looking in can hardly be doubted. The following are a more-or-less random sample of three genuine encounters, each of which reveals essentially the same view of the message of biology for our understanding of human behaviour. The first two encounters were engineered by one of the present authors; the third has been reported by Richard Dawkins (1982).

1. A college class is asked to consider what would be the consequences of discovering that certain racial differences in intellectual ability are 'biologically based'. Without having been told, they assume that the racial groups involved are whites and non-whites, that the differences involved concern the relative 'amounts' of intelligence possessed by each group, and that it is the black group that is found to be the less able. On the basis of this imaginary discovery, the class agrees that it is useless for members of the inferior group to take high-level courses in school or to aspire to those fields of work in which certain intellectual skills are important. What the discovery confirms, they say, is the inevitable intellectual inferiority of the non-white section of the population.

2. A clinical psychologist is asked to imagine what he would say to a man who had committed numerous rapes and who had been shown, by an unspecified but valid method, to have a 'genetic predisposition' to rape. He says, 'You're a miserable rotten person. You have a tendency to commit these terrible crimes. It's going to be very hard to control this tendency, but we may be able to help you keep out of situations that will trigger them.' Asked to imagine what he would say to a man who had committed the same crimes but who did not have the genetic

predisposition, the same psychologist replies, 'You're a miserable rotten person. You've learned to be that way because you had some unfortunate experiences when you were young, but we can help you unlearn what you've learned, so that you won't have to keep treating women in this way.' On reflection, the clinical psychologist acknowledges that his replies are based on assumptions about the imperviousness of 'biological' conditions to treatment, in contrast with the reversibility of learning.

3. A young woman stands up to question a sociobiologist at a conference. With great emotion, she asks whether there is evidence for genetic sex differences in human psychology. It takes an observer a moment or two to realize why she seems on the verge of tears; she believes an affirmative answer will seal her fate.

The stories biology can be made to tell are many and varied. They depend in part upon the particular branch of biology being studied, in part upon the aims, beliefs, and intentions of the teller, and in part upon the outlook and expectations of the listener. Sometimes, as in these three examples, the teller intends one thing and the listener hears something else; but frequently, teller and listener agree on what the message is. Time and again, the stories biology is made to tell contain messages of necessity and fate; and time and again, the stories the social sciences are made to tell contain messages of freedom and hope. From a logical and a biological point of view, both associations are totally arbitrary; but from an ideological point of view, they may be made to serve very explicit social and political purposes.

In Chapter 4, we saw that even careful anthropologists may find it difficult to get outside the cultures in which they grew up. Using a combination of their own critical skills and painstaking analysis, however, they attempt to monitor their own preconceptions and to see the worlds of others as clearly as they can. We can and should do the same for the world of science, whether or not we spend our professional lives in that world. This task will be a little easier if we can bring ourselves to stop expecting science to give us ultimate answers to the biggest questions of human existence: What is our true nature? What is the meaning of human life? Could the world be a better place than it is today? Our inability to distinguish myth from theory, one philosopher of science has observed, is bound up with the entanglement of 'the quest for knowledge' with 'the quest for security' (Toulmin 1982).

Neither optimism nor pessimism about the human condition stems directly from scientific analysis of past or present. Rather, each arises from the attitudes that we bring to such 'facts' as are available to us. In the end, it is doubtful whether either attitude is really of very much use to us; for both optimism and pessimism appear to represent little more than contrasting but equally unreflective assumptions about the nature of human possibilities. What we need is not blind confidence or blind despair, but rather a disciplined and wary sort of hope. In hope, we shall want to be informed about as many aspects of the human condition as bear on the task of creating a more peaceable world; but, by the same token, we shall want to reject all fatalistic forecasts, and particularly those that pass themselves off as the latest findings of science.

The conclusion to be drawn from our inquiry into the science and politics of aggression is not that there are pacific angels rather than aggressive monsters inside our heads. We are not fundamentally virtuous beings who have been led astray by evil, any more than we are fundamentally wicked creatures who have somehow stumbled upon good. Admittedly, certain kinds of theology claim to be able to tell us which is more real in us, good or evil. But any scientist who claims the same is stepping beyond Toulmin's quest for knowledge and setting out upon the quest for security; and we should not delude ourselves into taking for granted that he or she has any special expertise, or any suitable qualifications, for so bold an undertaking.

Can we make better use of the impressive scientific techniques available to us? We can, but only by taking responsibility for choosing and valuing in the uncertainty that always surrounds human activities. We are not devils in false finery, nor yet angels in rags; we are women and men in the world that makes us every moment and that we make and unmake in our thoughts and actions. Can we keep our constructions of aggression where they belong, serving us as we strive to understand our own behaviour and that of other animals so as to improve the immediate and long-range prospects for us all? We can, but only if we resist the temptation to project our hopes and fears onto our scientific constructs. For if we do so, it is merely our hopes and fears that we shall get back, writ large in the authoritative language of science. When that science is a branch of biology, the writing too often appears to be graven in stone, defining for us the very fate we should be defining for ourselves, as intelligently and as courageously as we can.

References

Alexander, R. D. (1979) *Darwinism and Human Affairs*. Pitman: London.

Archer, J. (1975) Rodent sex differences in emotional and related behavior. *Behavioral Biology* **14**, 451–79.

Archer, J. (1976) The organization of aggression and fear in vertebrates. In P. P. G. Bateson and P. H. Klopfer (eds), *Perspectives in Ethology*, Vol. 2, pp. 231–78. Plenum Press: New York.

Ardrey, R. (1961) *African Genesis*. Atheneum: New York.

Ardrey, R. (1966) *The Territorial Imperative*. Atheneum: New York.

Axelrod, R. (1984) *The Evolution of Cooperation*. Basic Books: New York.

Axelrod, R. and W. D. Hamilton (1981) The evolution of cooperation. *Science* **211**, 1390–6.

Bandura, A. (1969) Social-learning theory of identification processes. In D. Goslin (ed.), *Handbook of Socialization Theory and Research*, pp. 213–62. Rand McNally: Chicago.

Bandura, A. (ed.) (1971) *Psychological Modeling: Conflicting Theories*. Aldine-Atherton: New York.

Bard, P. (1934) Emotion: 1. The neurohumoral basis of emotional reactions. In C. A. Murchison (ed.), *A Handbook of General Experimental Psychology*, pp. 264–311. Clark University Press: Hanover, Mass.

Barlow, N. (ed.) (1933) *Charles Darwin's Diary of the Voyage of H.M.S. Beagle*. Cambridge University Press: Cambridge.

Bateson, M. C. (1972) *Our Own Metaphor*. Knopf: New York.

Bateson, P. P. G. (1982) Behavioural development and evolutionary processes. In King's College Sociobiology Group (ed.), *Current Problems in Sociobiology*, pp. 133–51. Cambridge University Press: Cambridge.

Bateson, P. P. G. (1983) Genes, environment and the development of behaviour. In T. R. Halliday and P. J. B. Slater (eds), *Animal Behaviour*, Vol. 3. *Genes, Development and Learning*, pp. 52–81. Blackwell: Oxford.

Beckstrom, J. H. (1985) *Sociobiology and the Law: The Biology of Altruism in the Courtroom of the Future*. University of Illinois Press: Urbana and Chicago.

Beckwith, J. (1976) Social and political uses of genetics in the United States: past and present. *Annals of the New York Academy of Sciences* **265**, 46–58.

Benton, D., P. F. Brain, and M. Haug (eds) (in press) *The Aggressive Female*. Eden Press: Montreal, Canada.

Blurton Jones, N. (ed.) (1972) *Ethological Studies of Child Behaviour*. Cambridge University Press: Cambridge.

Brain, C. K. (1981) *The Hunters or the Hunted? An Introduction to African Cave Taphonomy*. University of Chicago Press: Chicago and London.

Briggs, J. L. (1970) *Never in Anger: Portrait of an Eskimo Family*. Harvard University Press: Cambridge, Mass.

Brim, O. G. and J. Kagan (1980) (eds) *Constancy and Change in Human Development*. Harvard University Press: Cambridge, Mass.
Brockmann, H. J., A. Grafen, and R. Dawkins (1979) Evolutionarily stable nesting strategy in a digger wasp. *Journal of Theoretical Biology* **77**, 473–96.
Buss, A. H. and R. Plomin (1975) *A Temperament Theory of Personality Development*. Wiley: New York.
Campbell, D. (1975) On the conflicts between biological and social evolution and between psychology and moral tradition. *American Psychologist* **30**, 1103–26.
Cannon, W. B. and S. W. Britton (1925) Studies on the conditions of activity in endocrine glands. XV. Pseudaffective medulliadrenal secretion. *American Journal of Physiology* **72**, 283–94.
Caplan, A. L. (ed.) (1978) *The Sociobiology Debate: Readings on Ethical and Scientific Issues*. Harper & Row: New York.
Chagnon, N. and P. Bugos (1979) Kin selection and conflict: an analysis of a Yanomamo axfight. In N. Chagnon and W. Irons (eds), *Evolutionary Biology and Human Social Behavior: An Anthropological Perspective*, pp. 213–38. Duxbery: North Scituate, Mass.
Chorover, S. (1979) *From Genesis to Genocide: The Meaning of Human Nature and the Power of Behavior Control*. MIT Press: Cambridge, Mass.
Clutton-Brock, T. H. (1982) The functions of antlers. *Behaviour* **79**, 108–29.
Clutton-Brock, T. H. and S. D. Albon (1979) The roaring of red deer and the evolution of honest advertisement. *Behaviour* **69**, 145–70.
Clutton-Brock, T. H., F. E. Guinness, and S. D. Albon (1982) *Red Deer: Behaviour and Ecology of Two Sexes*. Edinburgh University Press: Edinburgh.
Cools, A. E. (1985) Brain and behavior: hierarchy of feedback system and control of its input. In P. P. G. Bateson and P. H. Klopfer (eds), *Perspectives in Ethology*, Vol. 6: *Mechanisms*, pp. 109–64. Plenum Press: London and New York.
Crabtree, J. M. and K. E. Moyer (1977) *Bibliography of Aggressive Behavior: a Reader's Guide to the Research Literature*. Alan R. Liss: New York.
Dart, R. (1954) The predatory transition from ape to man. *International Anthropological and Linguistic Review* **1**, 201–19.
Darwin, C. R. (1859) *The Origin of Species*. John Murray: London.
Darwin, C. R. (1871) *The Descent of Man, and Selection in Relation to Sex*, 2 vols, John Murray: London.
Darwin, C. R. (1872) *The Expression of the Emotions in Man and Animals*. John Murray: London.
Dawkins, R. (1976) *The Selfish Gene*. Oxford University Press: Oxford.
Dawkins, R. (1982) *The Extended Phenotype: The Gene as the Unit of Selection*. W. H. Freeman: Oxford and San Francisco.
Dawkins, R. (1985) Review of Steven Rose et al. (1984). *New Scientist*, 24 January, 59–60.
Dawkins, R. and J. R. Krebs (1979) Arms races between and within species. *Proceedings of the Royal Society of London*, B**205**, 489–511.
Delgado, J. M. R. (1964) Free behavior and brain stimulation. *International Review of Neurobiology* **6**, 349–449.
Delgado, J. M. R. (1965) Evolution of physical control of the brain. The James Arthur Lecture. American Museum of Natural History: New York.
Delgado, J. M. R. (1969) *Physical Control of the Mind: Towards a Psycho-Civilized Society*. Harper & Row: New York.

Delgado, J. M. R. (1981) Brain stimulation and neurochemical studies on the control of aggression. In P. F. Brain and D. Benton (eds), *The Biology of Aggression*, pp. 427–55. Sijthoff & Noordhoff: Alphen aan den Rijn, The Netherlands.

Delgado, J. M. R., V. Mark, W. Sweet, F. Ervin, G. Weiss, G. Bach-y-rita, and R. Hagiwara (1968) Intra-cerebral radio stimulation and recording in completely free patients. *Journal of Nervous and Mental Diseases* **147**, 329–40.

Dentan, R. K. (1979) *The Semai: A Nonviolent People of Malaysia* 2nd edn. Holt, Rinehart and Winston: New York. (First published 1968.)

Dickemann, M. (1979) Female infanticide, reproductive strategies and social stratification: a preliminary model. In Chagnon, N. and W. Irons (eds), *Evolutionary Biology and Human Social Behaviour: An Anthropological Perspective*, pp. 321–67. Duxbury: North Scituate, Mass.

Durant, J. R. (1985) The science of sentiment: the problem of the cerebral localization of emotion. In P. P. G. Bateson and P. H. Klopfer (eds), *Perspectives in Ethology*, Vol. 6: *Mechanisms*, pp. 1–31. Plenum Press: London and New York.

Eddington, A. S. (1930) *The Nature of the Physical World*, Cambridge University Press: Cambridge.

Eibl-Eibesfeldt, I. (1979) *The Biology of Peace and War: Men, Animals and Aggression*, Thames and Hudson: London.

Elseviers, D. (1974) XYY: Fact or Fiction?. *Science for the People* **6**, 22–4.

Evans, R. I. (1974) A conversation with Konrad Lorenz about aggression, homosexuality, pornography, and the need for a new ethic. *Psychology Today* **8** (6), 82–93.

Evans, R. I. (1975) *Konrad Lorenz: The Man and His Ideas*. Harcourt Brace Jovanovich: London and New York.

Feld, S. (1982) *Sound and Sentiment: Birds, Weeping, Poetics, and Song in Kaluli Expression*. University of Pennsylvania Press: Philadelphia.

Feshbach, S. (1970) Aggression. In P. H. Mussen (ed.), *Carmichael's Manual of Child Psychology*, Vol. 2, pp. 159–259. 3rd edn. Wiley: New York.

Flynn, J. P., H. Venegas, and S. Edwards (1970) Neural mechanisms involved in a cat's attack on a rat. In R. F. Whalen et al. (eds), *The Neural Control of Behavior*. Academic Press: New York.

Franz, S. I. (1912) New Phrenology. *Science* **35**, 321–8.

Freud, S. (1895) *The Project for a Scientific Psychology*. In Strachey (1966–74), Vol. 1, pp. 281–397.

Freud, S. (1923) *The Ego and the Id*. In Strachey (1966–74), Vol. 19, pp. 12–66.

Frodi, A., J. Macaulay, and P. R. Thome (1977) Are women always less aggressive than men? A Review of the Experimental Literature. *Psychological Bulletin* **84**, 634–60.

Fulton, J. F. (1949) *Functional Localization in the Frontal Lobes and Cerebellum*. Clarendon Press: Oxford.

Fulton, J. F. (1951) *Frontal Lobotomy and Affective Behavior: A Neurophysiological Analysis*. W. W. Norton: New York.

Fulton, J. F. and F. D. Ingraham (1929) Emotional disturbances following experimental lesions of the base of the brain (pre-chiasmal). *Journal of Physiology* **67**, xxvii–xxviii.

Fulton, J. F. and C. F. Jacobsen (1935) The functions of the frontal lobes, a comparative study in monkeys, chimpanzees and man. *Advances in Modern Biology* (Moscow) **4**, 113–23.

Galton, F. (1865) Hereditary talent and character. *Macmillan's Magazine* **12**, 157–66, 318–27.
Galton, F. (1869) *Hereditary Genius*. Macmillan: London.
Galton, F. (1883) *Inquiries into Human Faculty and its Development*. Reprinted for The Eugenics Society: London, 1951.
Ghiselin, M. T. (1974) *The Economy of Nature and the Evolution of Sex*. University of California Press: Berkeley.
Greenwood, D. J. (1984) *The Taming of Evolution: The Persistence of Nonevolutionary Views in the Study of Humans*. Cornell University Press: Ithaca and London.
Gruber, H. E. and P. H. Barrett (1974) *Darwin on Man*. Wildwood House: London.
Hamilton, W. D. (1964) The genetical evolution of social behaviour, Parts I and II. *Journal of Theoretical Biology* **7** 1–16, 17–52.
Hamilton, W. D. (1971) Selection of selfish and altruistic behavior in some extreme models. In J. F. Eisenberg and W. S. Dillon (eds), *Man and Beast: Comparative Social Behavior*, pp. 57–91. Smithsonian Institute Press: Washington, DC.
Hamilton, W. D. (1972) Altruism and related phenomena, mainly in social insects. *Annual Review of Ecology and Systematics* **3**, 193–232.
Hardin, G. E. (1956) Meaningless of the word protoplasm. *Science Monthly* **82**, 112–20.
Harlow, H. F. and M. K. Harlow (1965) The affectional systems. In A. M. Schrier, H. F. Harlow and F. Stollnitz (eds), *Behavior of Non-human Primates*, Vol. 2, pp. 287–334. Academic Press: New York and London.
Harré, R. (1979) *Social Being*. Blackwell: Oxford.
Harré, R. and P. F. Secord (1973) *The Explanation of Social Behaviour*. Blackwell: Oxford.
Hartup, W. W. (1974) Aggression in childhood: developmental perspectives. *American Psychologist* **29**, 336–41.
Hausfater, G. and S. B. Hrdy (1984) *Infanticide: Comparative and Evolutionary Perspectives*. Aldine: New York.
Hay, D. F. and H. S. Ross (1982) The social nature of early conflict. *Child Development* **53**, 105–13.
Heath, R. G., R. R. Monroe, and W. A. Micler (1955) Stimulation of the amygdaloid nucleus in a schizophrenic patient. *American Journal of Psychiatry* **73**, 127–9.
Heiligenberg, W. and U. Kramer (1972) Aggressiveness as a function of external stimulation. *Journal of Comparative Physiology* **77**, 332–40.
Hess, W. R. (1932–8). *Beiträge zur Physiologie des Hirnstammes*. I. G. Thieme: Leipzig.
Hess, W. R. (1954) *Diencephalon: Autonomic and Extrapyramidal Functions*. Greene: New York.
Hess, E. (1973) *Imprinting: Early Experience and the Developmental Psychobiology of Attachment*. Van Nostrand Reinhold: New York.
Hinde, R. A. (1960) Energy models of motivation. *Symposia of the Society for Experimental Biology* **14**, 199–213.
Hinde, R. A. (1974) *Biological Bases of Human Social Behaviour*. McGraw Hill: London and New York.
Hobbes, T. (1651) *Leviathan*. Crooke: London.

Hogan, J. A., S. Kleist, and C. S. L. Hutchings (1970) Display and food as reinforcers in the Siamese fighting fish (*Betta splendans*). *Journal of Comparative and Physiological Psychology* **70**, 35–357.

Hrdy, S. B. (1977) *The Langurs of Abu: Female and Male Strategies of Reproduction*. Harvard University Press: Cambridge, Mass. and London.

Humphrey, N. and R. J. Lifton (eds) (1984) *In a Dark Time*. Faber & Faber: London and Boston.

Isaac, G. Ll. (1983) Aspects of human evolution. In D. S. Bendall (ed.), *Evolution from Molecules to Men*, pp. 503–43. Cambridge University Press: Cambridge.

Jacob, F. (1983) Molecular tinkering in evolution. In D. S. Bendall (ed.), *Evolution from Molecules to Men*, 131–44. Cambridge University Press: Cambridge.

Jacobsen, C. F., J. B. Wolfe, and T. A. Jackson (1935) An experimental analysis of the functions of the frontal association areas in primates. *Journal of Nervous and Mental Diseases* **82**, 1–14.

Jarvik, L. F., V. Klodin, and S. Matsuyama (1973) Human aggression and the extra Y chromosome: fact or fancy? *American Psychologist* **28**, 674–82.

Keith, A. (1949) *A New Theory of Human Evolution*. Philosophers Library: New York.

Kevles, D. J. (1985) *In the Name of Eugenics: Genetics and the Uses of Human Heredity*. Knopf: New York.

King, H. E. (1961) Psychological effects of excitation of the limbic system. In D. E. Sheer (ed.), *Electrical Stimulation of the Brain*, pp. 477–86. University of Texas Press: Austin.

Kitcher, P. (1985) *Vaulting Ambition: Sociobiology and the Quest for Human Nature*. MIT Press: Cambridge, Mass. and London.

Klopfer, P. (1974) Instincts and chromosomes: what is an innate act? *American Naturalist* **103**, 556–60.

Koestler, A. (1967) *The Ghost in the Machine*. Hutchinson: London.

Koestler, A. and J. R. Smythies (eds) (1972) *Beyond Reductionism: New Perspectives in the Life Sciences*. Hutchinson: London.

Kohlberg, L. (1969) Stage and sequence: the cognitive-developmental approach to socialization. In D. A. Goslin (ed.), *Handbook of Socialization Theory and Research*, pp. 347–480. Rand McNally: Chicago.

Kohlberg, L. (1966) A cognitive-developmental analysis of children's sex-role concepts and attitudes. In E. Maccoby (ed.), *The Development of Sex Differences*, pp. 82–173. Stanford University Press: Stanford.

Kohlberg, L. (1981) Moral stages and moralization: the cognitive-developmental approach. In T. Lickona (ed.), *Moral Development and Behavior*, 31–53. Holt, Rinehart and Winston: New York.

Konner, M. (1982) *The Tangled Wing: Biological Constraints on the Human Spirit*. Holt, Rinehart and Winston: New York.

Lakoff, G. and M. Johnson (1981) *Metaphors We Live By*. University of Chicago Press: Chicago.

Leakey, R. E. (1981) *The Making of Mankind*. Michael Joseph: London.

Leakey, R. and R. Lewin (1977) *Origins*. Macdonald and Jane's: London.

Leakey, R. and R. Lewin (1979) *People of the Lake: Man; his Origins, Nature and Future*. Collins: London.

Le Boeuf, B. J. (1974) Male–male competition and reproductive success in elephant seals. *American Zoologist* **14**, 163–76.

Lee, R. B. and I. DeVore (eds) (1972) *Man the Hunter*. Aldine Press: Chicago.
Lehrman, D. S. (1953) A critique of Konrad Lorenz's theory of instinctive behavior. *Quarterly Review of Biology* **28**, 337–63.
Lehrman, D. S. (1970) Semantic and conceptual issues in the nature–nurture problem. In L. R. Aronson, E. Tobach, D. S. Lehrman, and J. S. Rosenblatt (eds), *Development and Evolution of Behavior*, pp. 17–52. W. H. Freeman: San Francisco.
Levine, L. (1958) Studies on sexual selection in mice. *American Naturalist* **92**, 21–6.
Lewis, C. (1942) *The Screwtape Letters*. G. Bles: London.
Lombardo, M. (1985) Mutual constraint in tree swallows: a test of the tit for tat model of reciprocity. *Science* **222**, 1363–5.
Long, M. (1980) Ritual and deceit. *Science Digest* **27**, 86–91.
Lorenz, K. Z. (1941) Comparative studies of the motor patterns of Anatinae. In Lorenz (1971), pp. 14–114.
Lorenz, K. Z. (1950) The comparative method in the study of innate behavior patterns. *Symposia of the Society for Experimental Biology* **4**, 221–68.
Lorenz, K. Z. (1966) *On Aggression*. Harcourt Brace Jovanovich: New York.
Lorenz, K. Z. (1971) *Studies in Animal and Human Behavior*, Vol. 1. Methuen: London.
Lumsden, C. J. and E. O. Wilson (1981) *Genes, Mind, and Culture*. Harvard University Press: Cambridge, Mass.
Maccoby, E. E. (1980) *Social Development: Psychological Growth and the Parent–child Relationship*, Harcourt Brace Jovanovich: New York.
McCord, J. (1979) Some child-rearing antecedents of criminal behavior in adult men. *Journal of Personality and Social Psychology* **37**, 1477–86.
McDougall, W. (1908) *An Introduction to Social Psychology*. Methuen: London.
McFarland, D. (1985) *Animal Behaviour: Psychobiology, Ethology and Evolution*. Pitman: London.
McGinnley, I. (1979) Androgens and the evolution of male gender identity among male pseudo-hermaphrodites with 5α-reductase deficiency. *New England Journal of Medicine* **300**, 1223–70.
MacLean, P. D. (1973) A triune concept of the brain and behavior. In T. Boag and D. Campbell (eds), *The Hincks Memorial Lectures, 1969*, pp. 4–66. University of Toronto Press: Toronto.
MacLean, P. D. (1982) On the origin and progressive evolution of the triune brain. In E. Armstrong and D. Falk (eds), *Primate Brain Evolution: Methods and Concepts*, pp. 291–316. Plenum Press, New York.
MacLean, P. D. and J. M. R. Delgado (1953) Electrical and chemical stimulation of frontotemporal portion of limbic system in the waking animal. *Electroencephalographic and Clinical Neurophysiology* **5**, 91–100.
Mark, V. H. and F. R. Ervin (1970) *Violence and the Brain*. Harper & Row: New York.
Maynard Smith, J. (1964) Group selection and kin selection. *Nature* **201**, 1145–7.
Maynard Smith, J. (1965) The evolution of alarm calls. *American Naturalist* **99**, 59–63.
Maynard Smith, J. (1974) The theory of games and the evolution of animal conflicts. *Journal of Theoretical Biology* **47**, 209–21.
Maynard Smith, J. (1983) Game theory and the evolution of cooperation. In D. S. Bendall (ed.), *Evolution from Molecules to Men*, pp. 445–56. Cambridge University Press: Cambridge.

Maynard Smith, J. and N. Warren (1982) Review of *Genes, Mind, and Culture* by C. J. Lumsden and E. O. Wilson. *Evolution* **36**, 620–7.

Miller, G. A., E. Galanter, and K. Pribram (1960). *Plans and the Structure of Behavior*. Henry Holt: New York.

Money, J. and A. A. Ehrhardt (1972) *Man and Woman, Boy and Girl*. Johns Hopkins University Press: Baltimore.

Moniz, E. (1936) *Tentatives Operatoires dans le Traitement de Certaines Psychoses*. Masson: Paris.

Montagu, A. M. F. (ed.) (1968) *Man and Aggression*. Oxford University Press: Oxford.

Montagu, A. M. F. (ed.) (1978) *Learning Non-Aggression*. Oxford University Press: New York and Oxford.

O'Callaghan, M. A. J. and D. Carroll (1982) *Psychosurgery: A Scientific Analysis*. MTP Press: Lancaster.

Olds, J. (1955) Physiological mechanism of reward. In M. R. Jones (ed.), *Nebraska Symposium on Motivation*, pp. 73–138. University of Nebraska Press: Lincoln.

Olioff, M. and J. Stewart (1978) Sex differences in the play behaviour of prepubescent rats. *Physiology and Behavior* **20**, 113–5.

Oyama, S. (1982) A reformulation of the idea of maturation. In P. P. G. Bateson and P. H. Klopfer (eds), *Perspectives in Ethology*, Vol. 5, pp. 101–31. Plenum Press: New York.

Oyama, S. (1985) *The Ontogeny of Information: Developmental Systems and Evolution*. Cambridge University Press: Cambridge.

Patterson, G. R. (1982) *Coercive Family Processes*. Castilia Press: Eugene, Oregon.

Piaget, J. (1965) *The Moral Judgement of the Child* (transl. by Marjorie Gabain). The Free Press: New York. (First published in English by Routledge and Kegan Paul, London, 1932.)

Piaget, J. and B. Inhelder (1969) *The Psychology of the Child*. Routledge and Kegan Paul: London.

Pittendrigh, C. S. (1958) Adaptation, natural selection, and behavior. In A. Roe and G. S. Simpson (eds), *Behavior and Evolution*, pp. 390–416. Yale University Press: New Haven.

Plotnik, R. (1974) Brain stimulation and aggression: monkeys, apes, and humans. In R. L. Holloway (ed.), *Primate Aggression, Territoriality, and Xenophobia: A Comparative Perspective*, pp. 389–415. Academic Press: New York.

Powers, W. T. (1973) *Behavior: The Control of Perception*. Aldine Press: Chicago.

Powledge, T. M. (1981) How not to study violence. In W. Gaylin, R. Macklin, R. Macklin, and T. M. Powledge (eds), *Violence and the Politics of Research*, pp. 49–140. Plenum Press: London and New York.

Pribram, K. H. and F. T. Melges (1969) Psychophysiological basis of emotion. In P. J. Vinken and G. W. Bruyn (eds), *Handbook of Clinical Neurology*, Vol. 3, pp. 316–42. Wiley Interscience: New York.

Pyeritz, R. et al. (1977) The XYY male: the making of a myth. In Ann Arbor Science for the People Editoral Collective, *Biology as a Social Weapon*, pp. 86–100. Burgess: Minneapolis, Minnesota.

Reader, J. (1981) *Missing Links: The Hunt for Earliest Man*. Collins: London.

Reynolds, V. (1976) *The Biology of Human Action*. W. H. Freeman: Reading and San Francisco.

Rose, S., R. C. Lewontin, and L. J. Kamin (1984) *Not in Our Genes: Biology, Ideology and Human Nature*. Penguin Books: Harmondsworth.

Schachter, S. and T. E. Singer (1962) Cognitive, social, and physiological determinants of emotional state. *Psychological Review* **69**, 379–97.

Schieffelin, E. I. (1976) *The Sorrow of the Lonely and the Burning of the Dancers*. St Martin's Press: New York.

Schieffelin, E. I. (1983) Anger and shame in the tropical forest: on affect as a cultural system in Papua New Guinea. *Ethos* **113**, 181–91.

Schneirla, T. C. (1956) Interrelationships of the 'innate' and the acquired in instinctive behavior. In *L'Instinct dans le Comportement des Animaux et les Hommes*, pp. 387–452. Masson: Paris.

Schneirla, T. C. (1966) Behavioral development and comparative psychology. *Quarterly Review of Biology* **41**, 283–302.

Scott, J. P. and J. L. Fuller (1965) *Genetics and the Social Behavior of the Dog*. University of Chicago Press: Chicago.

Searle, L. V. (1949) The organization of hereditary maze-brightness and maze-dullness. *Genetic Psychology Monographs* **39**, 279–335.

Sherman, P. W. (1980) The limits of ground squirrel nepotism. In G. W. Barlow and J. Silverberg (eds), *Sociobiology: Beyond Nature/Nurture?*, pp. 505–44. Westview Press: Boulder, Colorado.

Shettleworth, S. J. (1984) Learning and behavioral ecology. In J. R. Krebs and N. B. Davies *Behavioral Ecology: An Evolutionary Approach* (2nd edn), pp. 170–94. Sinauer: Sunderland, Mass.

Shields, W. M. and L. M. Shields (1983) Forcible rape: An evolutionary perspective. *Ethology and Sociobiology* **4**, 115–36.

Silverman, H. B. and H. J. Dunbar (1980) Aggressive tusk use by the narwhal (*Monodon monoceros* L.). *Nature* **284**, 57–8.

Smith, A. (1776) *An Inquiry into the Nature and Causes of the Wealth of Nations*. W. Strahan & T. Cadell: London.

Spradley, J. P. (1980) *Participant Observation*. Holt, Rinehart and Winston: New York.

Stannard, R. (1982) *Science and the Renewal of Belief*. SCM Press: London.

Steinmetz, S. K. (1977) *The Cycle of Violence: Assertive, Aggressive, and Abusive Family Interaction*. Praeger Special Studies: New York.

Steinmetz, S. K. and M. A. Straus (eds) (1974) *Violence in the Family*. Harper & Row: New York.

Stepansky, P. E. (1977) *A History of Aggression in Freud*. International University Press: New York.

Storr, A. (1970) *Human Aggression*. Penguin Books: Harmondsworth.

Strachey, J. (ed.) (1966–74) *The Standard Edition of the Complete Psychological Works of Sigmund Freud*, 24 vols. Hogarth Press: London.

Sulloway, F. J. (1979) *Freud, Biologist of the Mind*. Burnett Books in association with André Deutsch: London.

Sunday, S. R. and E. Tobach (eds) (1985) *Violence Against Women: A Critique of the Sociobiology of Rape*. Gordian Press: Staten Island, NY.

Symons, D. (1979) *The Evolution of Human Sexuality*. Oxford University Press: New York and Oxford.

Tanner, N. M. (1981) *On Becoming Human*. Cambridge University Press: Cambridge and New York.

Tanner, N. M. and A. L. Zihlman (1976) Women in evolution. 1. Innovation and selection in human origins. *Signs. Journal of Women in Culture and Society* **1**, 585–608.

Thomas, A. and S. Chess (1977) *Temperament and Development*. Brunner/Mazel: New York.
Thornhill, R. (1980) Rape in *Panorpa* scorpionflies and a general rape hypothesis. *Animal Behaviour* **28**, 52–9.
Thornhill, R. and N. W. Thornhill (1983) Human rape: an evolutionary analysis. *Ethology and Sociobiology* **4**, 137–73.
Time (1 August 1977) Why you do what you do, pp. 19–23.
Tinbergen, N. (1959) Comparative studies of the behavior of gulls (Laridae). In Tinbergen, *The Animal in its World: Explorations of an Ethologist, 1932–1972*, Vol. 1, pp. 25–98. Allen and Unwin: London.
Tinbergen, N. (1963) On aims and methods of ethology. *Zeitschrift für Tierpsychologie* **20**, 410–33.
Toates, F. M. (1980) *Animal Behaviour. A Systems Approach*. Wiley: Chichester and New York.
Toates, F. M. (1983) Models of Motivation. In T. R. Halliday and P. J. B. Slater (eds), *Animal Behaviour*, Vol. I: *Causes and Effects*, pp. 168–96. Blackwell: Oxford.
Toulmin, S. (1982) Scientific mythology. In S. Toulmin (ed.), *The Return to Cosmology*, pp. 21–85. University of California Press: Berkeley.
Trivers, R. (1985) *Social Evolution*. Benjamin Cummings: Menlo Park, California.
Tryon, R. C. (1940) Genetic differences in maze-learning ability in rats. *Yearbook of the National Society for the Study of Education* **39**, 111–19.
Valenstein, E. S. (1974) *Brain Control: A Critical Examination of Brain Stimulation and Psychosurgery*. Wiley: New York.
Valenstein, E. S. (1986) *Great and Desperate Cures*. Basic Books: New York.
van der Dennen, J. M. G. (1980) Problems in the concepts and definitions of aggression, violence, and some related terms. Polemologisch Instituut, Rijksuniversiteit. Gröningen.
van de Poll, N. E., H. H. Swanson, and H. G. van Oyen (1981) Gonadal hormones and sex differences in aggression in rats. In P. F. Brain and D. Benton (eds), *The Biology of Aggression*, pp. 243–52. Sijthoff and Noordhoff: Alphen aän den Rijn, the Netherlands.
van Hooff, J. A. R. A. M. (1972) A comparative approach to the phylogeny of laughter and smiling. In R. A. Hinde (ed.), *Non-Verbal Communication*, pp. 209–41. Cambridge University Press: Cambridge and New York.
van Hooff, J. A. R. A. M. (1967) The facial displays of the catarrhine monkeys and apes. In D. Morris (ed.), *Primate Ethology*, pp. 7–68. Weidenfeld and Nicolson: London.
Wender, P. H. (1971) *Minimal Brain Dysfunction in Children*. Wiley: New York.
Williams, G. C. (1966) *Adaptation and Natural Selection: A Critique of Some Current Evolutionary Thought*. Princeton University Press: Princeton, NJ.
Wilson, E. O. (1975) *Sociobiology: The New Synthesis*. Harvard University Press: Cambridge, Mass.
Wilson, E. O. (1978) *On Human Nature*. Harvard University Press: Cambridge, Mass.
Wilson, J. Q. and R. J. Herrnstein (1985) *Crime and Human Nature*. Simon and Schuster: New York.
Yarrow, M. R. and C. Waxler, et al. (1976) Dimensions and correlates of prosocial behavior in young children. *Child Development* **47**, 118–25.

Young, R. M. (1970) *Mind, Brain and Adaptation in the Nineteenth Century: Cerebral Localization and its Biological Context from Gall to Ferrier*. Clarendon Press: Oxford.

Young, R. M. (1985) *Darwin's Metaphor: Nature's Place in Victorian Culture*. Cambridge University Press: Cambridge and New York.

Zihlman, A. L. (1982) *The Human Evolution Coloring Book*. Harper and Row: New York.

Index